Charter Schools
and Accountability
in Public Education

Charter Schools and Accountability in Public Education

Paul T. Hill *and* Robin J. Lake
with Mary Beth Celio

BROOKINGS INSTITUTION PRESS
Washington, D.C.

Copyright © 2002
THE BROOKINGS INSTITUTION
1775 Massachusetts Avenue, N.W., Washington, D.C. 20036
www.brookings.edu

Library of Congress Cataloging-in-Publication data

Hill, Paul Thomas, 1943–
   Charter schools and accountability in public education / Paul T. Hill and
Robin J. Lake with Mary Beth Celio
      p. cm.
Includes bibliographical references (p.) and index.
   ISBN 0-8157-0266-3 (alk. paper)—ISBN 0-8157-0267-1 (pbk. : alk.
paper)
   1. Charter schools—United States—Evaluation. 2. Educational
accountability—United States. 3. Education—Standards—United States.
I. Lake, Robin J. II. Celio, Mary Beth. III. Title.
   LB2806.36.H54 2002
   371.01—dc21   2002005305

9 8 7 6 5 4 3 2 1

The paper used in this publication meets minimum requirements of the
American National Standard for Information Sciences—Permanence of
Paper for Printed Library Materials: ANSI Z39.48-1992.

Typeset in Sabon

Composition by AlphaWebTech
Mechanicsville, Maryland

Printed by R. R. Donnelley and Sons
Harrisonburg, Virginia

To Alice and Matthew

Foreword

The thirty-seven states and the District of Columbia that have charter school laws recognize that they have created a new kind of public entity—independently run schools of choice that are nonetheless publicly funded, open to all, and answerable to local school boards or state agencies. Unlike other public schools, which have little control over spending and teacher hiring, charter schools make these decisions for themselves.

In traditional public school systems, schools can survive and educators can keep their jobs even if large numbers of students fail to learn. Accountability is based on compliance with rules and avoidance of scandal. Because charter schools can be forced to close if they fail to benefit children, they pose unfamiliar problems of accountability. School boards need to monitor charter schools' progress closely so they can identify those that are failing students, and they need to develop options so they are not forced to leave students in schools that are not teaching effectively. They also need to judge the performance of many different schools, each of which has distinctive instructional methods and performance goals.

Charter school accountability also poses unfamiliar challenges for leaders of individual schools, which must both live up to their agreements with public authorizing agencies and, like private schools, maintain the confidence of parents and teachers.

Though the charter school movement is now more than seven years old, few public officials or school leaders have had to face these challenges. Most of the nation's twenty-three hundred charter schools are only in their first few years of operation, and only a small minority of the public agencies empowered to grant charters have ever done so.

This book is a first effort to understand how authorizing agencies and individual charter schools can solve complex accountability problems. These arrangements are under development on a daily basis, so no snapshot of current practice will be valid for long. Paul Hill and Robin Lake, therefore, seek to assist an ongoing process of problem solving, not to evaluate a fixed program. This book documents ways charter schools and government agencies approach accountability, and it traces the consequences of different accountability methods on schools' ability to pursue coherent instructional programs and serve families and children.

The results will serve three audiences: (1) charter school leaders and persons interested in seeking charters; (2) government officials, including leaders of charter authorizing agencies, state legislators, and governors interested in establishing or improving charter laws; and (3) elected officials and philanthropists willing to help charter schools. The authors hope that, in the long run, the study results might prove relevant to other public education reform efforts, including the standards-based reform movements present in every state. These movements can learn a great deal from charter schools about how to increase schools' freedom of action yet make sure they are held responsible for results.

The authors wish to thank the hundreds of individuals who were interviewed in the course of their research. They include charter school teachers, principals, governing board members, parents, and students, as well as local school board members, superintendents, central office administrators, staff of charter authorizing agencies, union leaders, local public officials and reporters, state education association heads and lobbyists, state education agency staff, state legislators and their assistants, state superintendents of public instruction, and aides to governors. This book tells their stories.

Christine Campbell, Paul Herdman, and Katrina Bulkley conducted most of the fieldwork on which this book is based and contributed to the analysis. Dean Millot and Larry Pierce contributed ideas throughout the many years Hill and Lake worked on the issue of charter schools. Paul Berman and his colleagues at RPP International helped throughout the study and provided indispensable data. James Harvey, Sarah Brooks, Julie Comiskey, and Abigail Winger of the University of Washington's Daniel J. Evans School of Public Affairs patiently read many draft chapters and made major contributions to the clarity, logic, and completeness of the final result.

At the Brookings Institution Press, Colleen McGuiness edited the text, Barbara Malczak proofread the pages, and Julia Petrakis provided an index.

The project was funded by the U.S. Department of Education, the Alcoa Foundation, New American Schools, the Pew Charitable Trusts, the Smith Richardson Foundation, the Joyce Foundation, and the Edna McConnell Clark Foundation.

The views expressed here are those of the authors and should not be ascribed to any of the persons acknowledged above or to the trustees, officers, or other staff members of the Brookings Institution.

MICHAEL H. ARMACOST
President

Washington, D.C.
April 2002

Contents

xi

Charter Schools
and Accountability
in Public Education

Charter Schools and Accountability

Charter schools are one of the most debated and least understood phenomena in American education. Like the blind men who described the elephant according to the part of it they touched, journalists and policy analysts write about charter schools as if they were many different things. Are charter schools devices for getting government funding for private education or a means of preserving public education? Do charter schools let educators teach in any way they like regardless of whether children learn, or do they make educators strictly accountable for performance?[1]

The root of the disagreement is accountability. Some people think that those who run charter schools are responsible only to adhere to professional standards and maintain a clientele of satisfied parents. Others think that those who run charter schools are responsible to show government and the general public that their children are learning what they need to become responsible, productive citizens. These differences of opinion do not split neatly on pro- versus anti-charter-school lines. Some people base their support of charter schools on the expectation that they will not have to answer to government, and others oppose charter schools on the basis of the same expectation. Similarly, some supporters think chartering creates a new performance-focused relationship between schools and government; and some opponents fear that a focus on school performance will weaken the government's ability to impose other agendas on schools.

I

This book is the result of the first national-scale study of charter school accountability. It explores charter school accountability both in theory and in fact. We hope it will inform elected officials, lay people interested in school reform, and educators about how public schools are held accountable, to whom, and for what.

We think this book has implications outside the charter school world for the national debate about school reform. Congress and forty-eight of the fifty state governments are struggling with the question of how to hold public schools accountable for student performance. Every prominent proposal for school reform—including site-based management initiatives sponsored by hundreds of school districts and voucher initiatives proposed by critics of government-run schools—aims at least in part to release schools from counterproductive regulatory burdens and to focus the efforts of students, teachers, and administrators on teaching and learning.

The most prominent such initiative is standards-based reform. Its logic is simple: Develop state standards for student performance in key subjects; test all students on whether they attain the standards; hold individual schools accountable for rates of student progress on the tests; and eliminate demands and constraints on schools that make it difficult for them to focus on effective instruction.

Standards-based reform starts at the top of the system by trying to align state goals, performance measures, and actions toward schools. Chartering starts at the bottom of the system, by creating freedom of action at the school level.

Despite these differences, chartering and standards-based reform have a great deal in common. Both impose a new obligation on government agencies—performance-based oversight of individual schools. Both try to deregulate schools so teachers and administrators can concentrate on serving students and raising achievement. Both make individual schools directly responsible to demonstrate student learning. These two reform initiatives—and other contemporary approaches such as vouchers and site-based management—can benefit students only if people within the schools learn how to use their freedom of action effectively and if people outside the schools learn how to judge performance without imposing unnecessary burdens.

The accountability problems of charters and standards-based reform are more alike than different. From the perspective of accountability, chartering and standards-based reform are best understood as complementary sides of one large school reform movement.

What Accountability Means for Charter Schools

We start with a very informal definition of accountability: A charter school is accountable to any entity or group whose support it must maintain to survive. Thus we considered charter schools accountable to government agencies, parents who can choose whether to enroll children in a charter school, teachers who can choose whether or not to work in a charter school, and community members who donate needed money, goods, and services. In general, we found that charter school leaders do take explicit account of the needs and expectations of all these groups. However, charter schools' relationships with different parties are not all equally well developed.

Most charter school leaders know that they must meet performance goals set by the government agencies that authorize them to receive public funds, and they must maintain a relationship of trust and confidence with those agencies. However, many government agencies have not clarified their expectations of and oversight processes regarding charter schools. Government agencies that do not clarify performance expectations send an implicit message that charter schools will ultimately be assessed on the basis of political popularity and compliance.

In addition to dealing with government authorizing agencies, most charter school leaders know that they must maintain relationships of trust and confidence with parents, teachers, and donors. Building these relationships, and reconciling the needs of different parties, is a major challenge that all charter schools struggle to meet. Charter schools that survive more than one or two years show signs of developing this capacity. They do so not by pandering to different groups but by making and keeping promises about what students will experience and learn. This establishes internal accountability—a belief that the school's performance depends on all adults working in concert, leading to shared expectations about how the school will operate, what it will provide children, and who is responsible for what.

Internal accountability can enable charter schools to meet ambitious performance expectations. But if government authorizers' expectations continue to be unpredictable and based on processes instead of outcomes, charter schools will be forced to focus on tasks other than the effective instruction of their students.

What Charter Schools Are

Charter schools are a new kind of institution, and not surprisingly even experts are having trouble figuring them out. A lay reader could easily find research reports and news articles characterizing charter schools in any number of ways. A recent Public Agenda report shows that the chaotic public discourse about charter schools has thoroughly confused parents, millions of whom simply do not know what charter schools are or what to think of them.[2]

Though state laws differ in detail, charter schools in general receive public funds, in a set amount for every child they enroll. Unlike conventional public schools, charter schools can decide how to spend their money—whom to hire, whether to have any full-time administrators, what books and equipment to buy, and what emphasis to put on technology. No child is required to attend a charter school, so all students enroll by choice. However, charter schools may not handpick their students, and schools with more applicants than spaces must conduct admissions lotteries.

In these ways charter schools are unlike conventional neighborhood public schools. But they are not fundamentally different from the magnet and specialty schools offered by virtually all large public school systems. Where charter schools are truly unique is in their accountability. Charter schools' relationships with government, parents, teachers, and community supporters are all different from conventional public schools' relationships with these entities.

Charter schools enter into performance agreements with local school boards or other state agencies (a charter is essentially a performance agreement) and if their students do not learn the schools can be denied any further public funds. In return for entering these performance agreements, charter schools are exempt from some regulations that apply to conventional public schools. State charter laws vary, but most schools are exempt from rules governing use of time during the school day and how teachers are chosen. Also unlike conventional public schools, charter schools do not automatically get free access to buildings. Most must rent space and pay for it from their own budgets. To bear these costs without drawing funds away from teaching and learning, many charter schools seek private donations of dollars or space.

A charter school must attract parents by making promises about what children will experience and learn, and if the school does not keep its promises, families are free to leave. Similarly, no teacher can be assigned to a charter school involuntarily. Because teachers are free to choose, the school must provide working conditions that capable teachers find attractive. If good teachers do not choose to work in a charter school, the school cannot deliver its instructional program; it then cannot fulfill its promises to the government agency that authorized it or to parents. Finally, because charter schools are often underfunded and must pay for their own space, most rely on voluntary contributions of money and services. Schools cannot get such donations without convincing community members and donors that children benefit.

Accountability is the focus of controversy about charter schools. Some people think that needing to satisfy parents, teachers, and donors as well as government is good for schools and can make them both more effective and more responsive. Others think the need to respond to parents, teachers, and donors as well as government makes charter schools unaccountable and thus, if not completely private, not fully public either.

The Meaning of Accountability in Public Education

Accountability is a word that is frequently used in connection with public education but is seldom carefully defined. In most settings, accountability is the relationship between a principal, a person who needs a task done and can pay to get it done, and an agent, who accepts responsibility for accomplishing the task in return for some form of payment.[3] This definition should be broad enough to apply to all settings, including public education. With respect to public education, most people can agree on who is the agent; it is the school or, in some instances, the teacher. However, people disagree strongly over who should be considered the principal in public education. (The term *principal* here does not refer to the head of a school but to the legal person for which the school acts as an agent.)

Is the principal in public education the government, represented by the local school board or some other agency? Or is the principal the parents, who are responsible for their children's health, safety, growth, and emotional and moral development? Or is it the community, whose orderliness and prosperity will depend on the children's development and whose taxes pay for education? These questions are difficult to answer because each of these entities is concerned about whether children learn what is required to earn a living and be good neighbors and citizens. However, these parties often disagree about what children need to learn and how schools can be operated. All of them have their own interests, which are sometimes not entirely consistent with those of children.

The theory of democratic accountability holds that a public school is a subordinate unit in a bureaucracy that executes policies enacted by elected officials.[4] Under this theory, elected officials are the principal for whom a public bureaucracy, and ultimately the school as a unit of that bureaucracy, act as agents. The adults who run a school are supposed to implement policies set by elected officials. Though teachers and principals are expected to use their professional expertise, they must do so within boundaries set by rules that are politically determined. Parents and community members can influence these policies by voting in elections and by petitioning officials for changes. Parents and community members can also build collaborative relationships with teachers and principals, but they cannot expect school staff to violate policies set by elected officials and higher levels of the bureaucracy.

Charter schools are one of two contemporary challenges to the traditional bureaucratic theory of democratic accountability. The other challenger is standards-based reform.

Both charters and standards-based reform retain government as a principal, but both constrain government. In the case of charter schools, elected officials and the administrators who work for them are able to decide what schools will be authorized to receive public funds, and they can cancel the charters of schools that do not meet their performance agreements. But elected officials may not make new rules whenever they please or unilaterally alter or cancel an agreement with a school that is performing as promised. In the case of standards-based reform, elected officials, and the administrators who work for them, set standards of student performance that each school must meet. Officials and administrators can intervene in schools that do not teach children to meet the standards. But elected officials are not supposed to impose new mandates that distract teachers and principals from the work of teaching students to meet the standards.

The charter school idea diverges from the standard model of democratic accountability in two additional ways. First, it tries to make parents, teachers, and community members co-principals, along with government. Each of these entities can deal directly with individual schools: the parents by deciding whether to enroll their children; teachers by deciding whether to work in the school; community members by deciding whether to provide direct support, including money, services, and goods, to individual schools; and government by deciding which schools to authorize to receive public funds. Second, it tries to make the adults in a school partners in a shared enterprise, not bureaucratic functionaries. Teachers and administrators work in charter schools by choice, and they stand to benefit (by keeping their jobs and enjoying freedom from regulation) if their school performs well and to suffer (by losing their jobs and possibly their reputations) if the school performs poorly.

In theory, parents, community members, and financial supporters who believe in a charter school also have something to gain if it survives and something to lose if it does not. These parties both have expectations of the school and take some responsibility for its performance. Charter schools therefore experience strong pressures to develop internal accountability, in which administrators, teachers, parents, and members expect things of one another and face expectations in return.

Democratic Accountability Is Problematic for Schools

Charter schools and standards-based reform have challenged traditional democratic accountability because of widespread dissatisfaction with elected officials as the sole principal for public schools. Teachers and principals complain that elected officials constantly impose new rules in response to political pressure and legislative negotiations, forcing constant reallocation of school resources and adjustment of teaching practices. Parents complain that politically set rules make schools unresponsive and unable to adjust to the needs of individual children. Many elected officials sympathize with these complaints and think that oversight by political decisionmaking bodies has made schools much less efficient and responsive than they could be.

Though elected officials are the representatives of the people who vote them into office, the policies they make about public schools do not reliably reflect the needs of schools and children. In some instances the failures of representative bodies might be due to personal weaknesses of elected officials. But the problem is more structural than personal. Representative bodies enact policies that apply to all schools, but the needs of children are diverse. Schools struggle with rules that were not made with them in mind but which they must follow nonetheless. Moreover, as Terry E. Moe has shown, groups that win enactment of policies that favor themselves are usually able to protect those policies even when they no longer have majority support.[5] Thus policies accumulate over time and the adults who work in schools must follow many of them, including some that only a few people continue to support and that conflict with one another.

The results can be seen most vividly in the central offices of big-city school districts. These have many separate sub-bureaucracies, each responsible to ensure that schools comply with a particular set of federal, state, or local school board rules. School leaders must comply with the rules administered by each of these offices. This arrangement is often called fragmented centralization. It focuses school leaders' energy on relationships with the central office and limits the time they have to lead their school's instructional program. Schools that get funds from many federal and state programs must follow various regulations about how money can be used, which students are allowed to receive services funded by what programs, and which teachers are allowed to serve particular students.[6]

No one thinks fragmented centralization is a good thing. But some analysts fear that the challenge charter schools pose to traditional democratic accountability is itself undemocratic. People who favor charter schools and standards-based reform argue that a democratic society can choose to do its business in many ways. They point to many circumstances in which the United States constrains political oversight and sets up institutions that can exercise a great deal of discretion: Consider the Securities and Exchange Commission, the Federal Reserve System, and developers of secret weapons. Like the judicial system, which is also insulated from detailed political oversight, the effectiveness of these enterprises depends on being able to sustain consistent actions. Such institutions are compatible with democracy because they ultimately depend on the results of elections and the support of elected officials. They can be changed, albeit slowly, by sustained pressures from determined majorities.

Democratic societies can also give individuals and institutions great discretion over the use of public funds. No one thinks it violates democratic principles to allow government-paid air traffic controllers to decide how many planes can land in a particular hour or to let military commanders keep some of their plans secret.

Thus alternatives to the strict hierarchy of democratic accountability can be just as democratic. Schools, like other vital public enterprises, must have enough freedom of action to perform competently. They need not be forced to advance the political objectives of whatever party controls a legislative majority, seek bureaucratic approvals for every action, or put the completion of paperwork above the delivery of their core service. Public institutions must ultimately answer to the voters and elected officials, but they must be insulated from day-to day-politics. That is why Congress invented independent regulatory commissions and made it impossible for a new president to totally reconstitute the Federal Reserve System Board of Governors.

For similar reasons, state legislatures gave charter schools substantial freedom of action, but they provided mechanisms for periodic and focused, but nonetheless consequential, public oversight. The charter school movement does not intend to remove public education from its democratic roots. But it does challenge the assumption that democracy requires a trade-off between accountability and effectiveness.

Assessing the Consequences of New Accountability for Public Education

Charter schools and standards-based reform are reactions to the poor performance of rules-driven public schools. But the new forms of account-

Figure 1-1. *Theory of Charter School Accountability*

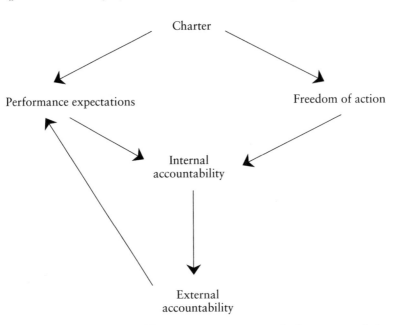

ability bring their own problems. Critics are particularly concerned about charter schools, fearing that public officials will be too lenient in allowing incompetent groups to obtain charters and continuing to fund even very low performing schools. Critics also fear that the heads of charter schools might abuse their powers, tyrannizing teachers, gulling parents, and falsifying data about their school performance. Finally, many are concerned that the parent- and teacher-choice elements of the charter school idea will lead charter schools to exclude the hard-to-teach and create enclaves of privilege.

As was the case with traditional democratic accountability, these alternatives to it might have hidden costs and might work in unexpected ways. No one can tell for sure a priori.

Figure 1-1 summarizes the theory of charter school accountability. A charter both establishes a school's freedom of action (by giving it control of decisions about spending, staffing, schedules, and so on) and creates pressure for performance (via student learning goals negotiated with the school's authorizer and the expectations of parents, teachers, and community supporters). The combination of resource control and performance pressure leads the school to develop internal accountability—divisions of labor and mutual expectations that make the school an effective learning environment for children. Internal accountability allows the school to perform as promised and thus to be accountable to its principals—government, parents, teachers, and donors.

A drawing of the theory of accountability under standards-based reform would look somewhat different. It would, however, include the key elements of figure 1-1: performance expectations, school freedom of action, and internal accountability leading to external accountability.

These new conceptions of accountability for public schools are theories, not necessarily facts. This book represents an early effort to understand how new forms of accountability for public education work. The book's main focus is on charter schools, which, though relatively new, have far more fully functioning exemplars than standards-based reform. Though all but two states are formally committed to standards-based reform, it is being designed and rolled out very slowly. The vast majority of states are still working on defining standards and deciding how to measure student performance.

With the help of a contract from the U.S. Department of Education and several foundations, we set out to explain how charter school accountability works in practice.[7] We designed our research around the ideas in figure 1-1: inquiring about how charter schools come to understand the expectations of schools' government, parents, teachers, and donors; how charter schools develop internal accountability; and how internal accountability facilitates external accountability.

The study focused on six states—Arizona, California, Colorado, Georgia, Massachusetts, and Michigan. We selected these states for three reasons: (1) they contain the vast majority of charter schools in existence for at least three years; (2) they represent the major differences in state charter school laws; and (3) they provide examples from all the major regions of the country—West, Northeast, South, Southwest, and Midwest. Differences in state laws are important. Arizona, for example, has an extremely permissive state charter law, whereas California's and Georgia's are much more restrictive. Massachusetts has demonstrated a strong commitment to helping its charter schools succeed; Michigan officials are deeply divided about the desirability of charter schools.

We studied a total of 150 schools and 60 authorizing agencies in these states. We conducted extensive case studies of internal accountability relationships in 17 of the 150 schools, interviewing school principals, teachers, other staff members, parents, governing board members, and authorizing agency officials.[8] We also interviewed state legislators and their aides, governors' aides, senior staff of state education agencies, administrators responsible for issuing regulations and guidelines for charter schools, individuals designated to approve charter schools or hear appeals when local districts rejected charter school applications, charter school assistance organization heads, and senior staff members of other education associations that attempted to influence policy regarding charter schools.

In addition, we supplemented the results of state and school case studies with data from a nationally representative survey of charter schools. As we planned our study, RPP International of Emeryville, California, was starting a national survey of charter schools, under contract with the U.S. Department of Education.[9] We were fortunate to be able to contribute accountability questions to the RPP International surveys. As we analyzed our fieldwork data, we also analyzed the national data files generated by RPP International's surveys.[10]

From these sources we learned a great deal about accountability in the charter school movement. We were also exposed to many ideas that went well beyond the original intent of our study, insights that we thought deserved a broader audience than a government report, no matter how good, typically earns.

CHAPTER TWO

Charter Laws and Politics

Legislators start the conversation about charter school accountability, but school boards, administrators, and the charter schools themselves ultimately define it. The exact terms of the state charter school law matter. But so do the actions of the state and local agencies that solicit and review applications from people who want to run charter schools. These agencies act politically, in response to pressures from parents, unions, public school administrators, and others—some encouraging applications and supporting charter schools, and others discouraging applications and paying as little attention as possible to charter schools. Finally, a charter school ultimately interprets both the legal requirements and the expectations of the entities that enact, administer, support, and oppose the charter school law. Because laws are seldom crystal clear, and the positions of administrative agencies and interest groups are constantly evolving, charter schools face a complex legal and political environment. The following tensions are a typical result.

—Under most state laws, charter schools are supposed to be freed from regulatory constraints to produce better results, but they often must negotiate away those freedoms to gain sponsorship from school districts that view them as a threat.

—Some laws say that charter school accountability should be defined by the school's contract, but implementation is left to district or state middle managers who believe that charter schools should be held to all the same state and local accountability rules as other public schools.

—Charter schools are expected to innovate but, at the same time, media coverage and political focus on high-stakes standardized tests create pressure for conservative, proven approaches.

While studying how accountability is functioning in our case studies and in our reviews of the first thirty-four charter laws, we found that

—State charter school accountability practice is the result of a mixture of statutory language and implementation arrangements. One constrains and molds the other, but no simple direct correlation says a given state law produces a given accountability relationship.

—The political and implementation process can create confusion and inconsistency, sending mixed messages to schools about what results they are responsible for.

Constraints and Opportunities for Accountability

Charter school laws create alternative legal frameworks for organizing public schools. In the place of district-run schools, charter school laws establish a system of schools that operate according to a charter or contract between a public authorizing agency and an independent school operator. In theory, charter schools are freed from rules and regulations and then are held strictly accountable for results defined in the charter. This basic bargain of autonomy for accountability defines public charter schools and distinguishes them from alternative public schools or vouchers. But the thirty-four charter laws we studied and the states we visited operate on many different dimensions of this theory.

The law itself is the best starting place for understanding why states differ in their basic accountability frameworks.

—It creates authority for agencies to charter schools; that is, by allowing only school districts to charter or limit the number of schools, thereby limiting market competition.

—It establishes levels of flexibility from state and local laws and regulations.

—It sets some guidelines for how schools should be judged; that is, by allowing authorizing agencies limited discretion or by requiring that charter schools meet state standards and so on.

The laws begin to define charter schools' accountability relationships with authorizing agencies, other state agencies, families, and professional interests.

Accountability to Authorizing Agencies

Charter school laws make a charter school accountable to its authorizing agency, which is a local school board or another public agency approved by the state. Charter schools are held accountable to approving authorities by the requirements to become a charter school, the monitoring of a school's ongoing operations, and the possibility of charter revocation or renewal.

No one has a right to operate a charter school. Interested providers have to apply to obtain a charter to operate a public school with public funds. Most state charter school laws list the elements that applicants must address in their charter school applications. These include descriptions of the school's education program, details about the school's financial and management plans, a plan for self-governance (who is responsible for oversight of the school's day-to-day operations), and criteria for revocation and renewal of the school's contract.

The purpose of the application requirements is to increase the likelihood that schools receiving charters are good schools that serve the public interest. The application also structures the contract that allows the school to operate with public funds and sets the conditions for the renewal or termination of the charter.

In addition to reviewing and deciding on whether to issue a school charter, authorizing agencies are charged by state law to monitor the charter school contract. This is done in two ways. Authorizers are required to take steps to review a school's compliance with the terms of its contract and other applicable state laws. State laws also require charter schools to submit regular audits and reports to their authorizers, other state agencies, and the public.

Finally, a charter school is held accountable to the authorizing agency by the legal power given to chartering agencies to terminate a charter if it fails to achieve its contractual commitments. Statutory details about the renewal process vary among the states.

Accountability to Other State Agencies

Charter schools are never fully exempt from the laws and regulations affecting other public schools. To the extent that charter schools must comply with these requirements, they are also accountable to government agencies in addition to the agency approving their charter. Even charter school laws that provide for blanket waivers from the state education code, presumably to give them autonomy to improve student teaching and learning, call on charter schools to meet requirements for the health, safety, and civil rights of their students. Some states (for example, Michigan) require charter schools to meet all regulations that apply to other schools, but most exempt charter schools from some or all regulations. Other states leave the determination of what charter schools are required to do to the state board of education. Most statutes are vague on this issue, which leaves room for state agencies, especially when under pressure by interest groups, to impose additional regulatory requirements on charter schools.

Accountability to Families and Professional Interests

In theory, charter laws can make schools accountable in many directions: to the broader community, to families, to teachers and others who pro-
'e instruction, and to groups representing professional standards.

Charter school laws seek to restore a balance between the private and
ublic interests in education. They recognize the private interest in schooling by allowing families to choose among schools that take different approaches to education.

Charter schools must attract administrators and teachers. Though schools will also have choices about whom they employ, their capacity to hire and maintain high-quality staffs will depend on pay, working conditions, and institutional reputation. Under such conditions, schools will need to maintain their reputations as secure and satisfying places to work. Potential staff members might assess schools according to criteria similar to those used by parents or the school board. However, schools based on unsound educational theories or burdened by poor management might be sanctioned by the departure of essential staff members even sooner than they are abandoned by parents and the school board. Similarly, charter schools that gain good reputations among teachers will probably earn parental and board support because of positive mentions by teachers.

Many charter schools will join voluntary networks of like-minded schools for the purpose of sharing knowledge and making efficient joint investments in teacher training and assessment. Some of these new charter networks might operate, as do some private school networks, as inspectorates, alerting their managers and boards to declines in instructional quality.[1] As Anthony S. Bryk has suggested, school districts and other charter authorizing agencies might also fulfill their oversight responsibilities by creating inspectorates intended to identify school performance problems and charter schools that need help or other intervention.[2]

Four Charter School Theories

Despite the variation in specific elements of state charter school laws, our interviews with those who wrote or promoted the original laws in our case study states in addition to our review of the first thirty-four laws have led us to identify four general strategies, or theories of action, most often pursued within the charter school movement. We describe these strategies as the innovation/experimentation strategy, the standards-based reform strategy, the new supply of public schools strategy, and the competition/market strategy. These four strategies are distinct but not mutually exclusive. Many charter laws are amalgams of two or more of these theories. The strategies should also not be considered exhaustive, only the most common.

The Innovation/Experimentation Strategy: Create new schools to serve as laboratories for successful teaching strategies. (Theory #1)

A few states have enacted charter school laws that are intended to create special or magnet schools within existing school districts. Georgia, for example, provides charter status, giving schools added flexibility and a structure for setting school improvement goals. Georgia legislators were either not interested or able, however, to pass a law that changed the dominant position of local school boards over all schools. Georgia charter schools, for instance, have some freedom to adjust curriculum and employ staff, but they look very much like a traditional public school. The charter schools have access to federal and some foundation start-up funds. To become a charter school, they must submit a school improvement plan to the district and obtain the support of teachers and parents for the plan. In almost every other way they look like other district schools. The local school district still operates the school, and students usually are assigned to the school. Staff are generally chosen, assigned, evaluated, and paid by the district; the district still controls virtually all spending and purchasing; and the district has considerable say over the charter schools' instructional strategies. For the most part, the accountability expected of charter schools is the same as other district schools and is heavily weighted toward compliance with state and local rules.

The Standards-Based Reform Strategy: Free schools from rules so they can meet higher expectations. (Theory #2)

By making charter schools a part of a state's standards-based reform program, they are seen as one of several tools for helping students achieve higher standards. The laws are usually designed to permit local districts to create new schools serving students who have not been well served in conventional public schools. They may be students with different learning styles or students whose parents want a more traditional, back-to-basics program. Charter schools in these states also serve many alternative students or students at risk of falling through the cracks of existing schools. Again, the purpose of these charter laws is not to provide an alternative framework for providing education, but to increase options within the existing district-run system of public education. In some, but not all, cases, charter schools are still legally an arm of the school district, not their own legal entity. Many services are provided by the district, and in many ways the schools are treated like other public schools. Focus on accountability is both on student performance and on compliance with state and local laws and regulations. In our sample, California and Colorado fall into this group.[3]

The New Supply of Public Schools Strategy: Open the system up to a set of new school providers. (Theory #3)

Some charter school laws set out to create an alternative framework for providing public education. Chartering authority is vested in state agencies or groups that are separate from the local school districts. Community groups, nonprofits, and, in some cases, for-profit groups are authorized to obtain charters and run schools. Funding usually flows directly from the state to the charter school, and each school is held accountable for performance to its independent chartering agency. Charter schools in new supply states operate independently of local boards. They decide on the curriculum and whom to employ. Accountability is provided through the monitoring of the authorizing agency for faithfulness to the terms of the contract and by the choice of parents to have their children attend the schools. Michigan and Massachusetts are states with laws of this kind.

The Competition/Market Strategy: Let parent choice drive the entire system to improve. (Theory #4)

States such as Arizona have passed charter school laws that are designed to provide an alternative system to the current district-run system and to actively compete with that system. The dominant value of this market-based approach is parent choice. Advocates of this strategy generally assert that parents are in the best position to choose what is best for their children and their choices should directly influence the kinds of instruction and allocation of funds for public schools. Market-based laws try to increase the range of schooling options available to parents. The government role in this model is to stimulate creation of a large supply of new schools and provide information to help inform parent choice. Laws that follow this strategy allow many different agencies to sponsor schools to ensure that no one agency will turn down an application for political reasons. Instead of trying to create a smaller number of carefully selected schools, the sponsors generally assume that the market will serve as the primary accountability mechanism. In Arizona, the state's two major authorizing boards license schools that meet minimum requirements to provide educational programs and receive public funds based on the number of students enrolled.

Inconsistent Laws

The four strategies or theories provide a starting point for understanding the implied accountability methods. However, as Hubert H. Humphrey once said, "Making laws is like making sausage." The political process is rife with a wide variety of specialized interest group concerns and outright political gaming that make it unlikely a coherent law will result from a particular philosophy about the purpose of charter schools.

Table 2-1. *Stated Purposes of the Charter School Laws*

Purpose of law	States
Offer diverse approaches to teaching and learning; opportunities for innovation (Theory #1)	California, Colorado, Delaware, District of Columbia, Florida, Louisiana, Idaho, Illinois, Kansas, Massachusetts, Michigan, Minnesota, Nevada, New Hampshire, New Jersey, North Carolina, Ohio, Pennsylvania, Rhode Island, South Carolina, Utah, Virginia, Wyoming
Improve pupil achievement (Theory #2)	Arizona, California, Colorado, Delaware, District of Columbia, Florida, Idaho, Illinois, Kansas, Massachusetts, Michigan, Minnesota, Nevada, New Hampshire, New Jersey, North Carolina, Ohio, Pennsylvania, Rhode Island, South Carolina, Utah, Wyoming
Provide new professional opportunities for teachers (Theory #1)	California, Colorado, District of Columbia, Florida, Idaho, Illinois, Kansas, Louisiana, Massachusetts, Michigan, Minnesota, Nevada, New Hampshire, New Jersey, North Carolina, Ohio, Pennsylvania, Rhode Island, South Carolina, Utah, Virginia, Wyoming
Create additional choices for parents and students (Theory #4)	Arizona, California, Colorado, District of Columbia, Indiana, Illinois, Delaware, Florida, New Jersey, North Carolina, Massachusetts, Michigan, Pennsylvania, Rhode Island, South Carolina, Utah, Virginia, Wyoming
Develop new forms of accountability (Theory #2)	California, Colorado, District of Columbia, Delaware, Florida, Idaho, Illinois, Louisiana, Massachusetts, Michigan, Minnesota, Nevada, New Hampshire, New Jersey, North Carolina, Pennsylvania, Rhode Island, South Carolina, Utah

Sometimes charter laws are enacted by strange bedfellows who do not reveal their real intentions so they can preserve a diverse coalition in support of the proposed legislation. For example, supporters of school vouchers often back charter school legislation as a first step to future deregulation and privatization of K–12 education, while others see charters as a stopgap to avoid vouchers. Opponents of charter schools often insist that a charter school bill include provisions that will blunt its potential impact on school districts and teachers unions, such as requiring all teachers to be certified or providing financial compensation for districts that lose students to charter schools. Even the most originally coherent laws become watered down, negotiated, and tinkered with during deliberations. As a result, the purpose of the law, as well as the elements of the law that support that purpose, is often inconsistent.

Table 2-1. *continued*

Purpose of law	States
Establish new tools for measuring student performance (Theory #1)	Colorado, District of Columbia, Delaware, Florida, Louisiana, Minnesota, Nevada, New Hampshire, New Jersey, North Carolina, Utah
Create new opportunities for specific populations, such as at-risk or gifted (Theory #3)	California, Colorado, Florida, Illinois, Kansas, Michigan, Nevada, New Jersey, North Carolina, Rhode Island
Create performance-based educational programs in place of rules and regulations (Theory #2)	Arkansas, California, District of Columbia, Georgia, Massachusetts, Mississippi, South Carolina, Virginia
Encourage parent and community involvement (Theory #4)	Colorado, Illinois, Rhode Island, South Carolina, Utah
Create avenues for new providers to start schools; create alternatives to traditional public education (Theory #3)	Illinois, Kansas, Louisiana, Nevada, Rhode Island
Establish school as the unit for improvement (Theory #2)	District of Columbia, Florida, Illinois, Michigan, New Hampshire, New Jersey
Add deregulation— freedom from rules and regulations (Theory #1)	District of Columbia, Kansas, Nevada, New Hampshire, Rhode Island

The stated purposes of the first thirty-four charter laws and the guiding theory with which the intent most closely aligns are presented in table 2-1. The intent sections of laws are usually not a true reflection of the sponsors' intent, but they do guide judicial interpretation of the statute. The fact that most states list multiple purposes, aligned with multiple theories, is also an important reflection of the need to satisfy diverse interests and to make compromises in the political process.

The political process churns out more than mixed signals about the purpose of the law. Accountability provisions of the law are often similarly vague or misaligned within a particular piece of legislation.

Slightly more than half the states give charter schools blanket waivers, under which schools are accountable only for the terms of their charters plus health, safety, and civil rights requirements, leaving interpretation to state and local agencies.[4] However, other provisions of the same laws can open up the possibility that charter schools are subject to all the requirements that apply to public schools. These ambiguities are certainly the result of legislative compromises permitting all contending factions to insert some language they like.

California's law, for example, intended to free charter schools to meet state standards by whatever methods and strategy they could develop. But by requiring schools to negotiate with their sponsor district for that flexibility, it was often compromised. Many California charter schools do not have freedom to hire and fire staff or to determine fully how they spend their funds. Thus many California schools do not have the flexibility envisioned by proponents that would allow them to make great progress toward meeting new achievement targets. Some states, including California, have succeeded in clarifying some aspects of their charter laws, but only at the expense of new provisions whose meaning will become clear only in practice.

In addition, different parties have different ideas about how charter school progress should be measured. On the one hand, if the major focus is performance on standardized tests, those looking for instructional innovation are likely to be disappointed. On the other hand, if the state is more concerned about choice and limits a school's accountability to the proper handling of public funds and satisfying parents, those looking for improved student test scores may be dissatisfied.

The lack of clarity in law—compounded by the politics of implementation—creates a difficult environment for policymakers, researchers, and the general public to understand and evaluate charter school accountability. As well, schools find themselves in the difficult position of having to please many different actors who are interested in diverse results.

Essential Questions Remain

The legal structure for charter school accountability is complex and varied among all the states with charter school laws. All charter school laws require more than performance on standardized tests to obtain and keep a charter. In most states, however, the laws are rarely specific and are often schizophrenic about how accountability will work in practice. This leaves responsibility for establishing an accountability framework for charter schools to state departments of education or charter school authorizing agencies or both. The following questions are critical: How do these frameworks evolve in practice? How do charter schools balance or prioritize competing demands for accountability? How do state agencies responsible for oversight implement the law? How do state politics and history shape how laws are enforced and interpreted?

CHAPTER THREE

Internal
Accountability

Chartering puts schools in a unique set of interdependent relationships. Unlike conventional public schools, charter schools must attract parents and teachers who can choose other schools, and they must enter directly into relationships with private organizations that provide financial support, advice, and services. Unlike private schools, they must negotiate their charters with public authorizing agencies, convince the same agencies that they are fulfilling their charters, and build a relationship of trust and confidence in anticipation of charter renewal.

To meet all these obligations, schools must be able to discipline their internal work. The needs to maintain relationships of trust and confidence with the government agencies that authorize them and to retain the support of independent members of their own governing boards as well as of teachers and parents motivate intense internal collaboration that leads to internal accountability. Control over spending and staffing decisions makes internal accountability possible.

Charter schools' relationships with government authorizers and other external actors affect the ways teachers, administrators, and other internal actors work together.

—Individual school governing boards (the legal persons that receive charters and act as stewards of individual schools' missions and identities) are important new actors in public education. They often, but not invariably, provide the oversight that makes school staff accountable.

—Charter schools are alert to the need to maintain parents' confidence, though parents seem more focused on matters of caring and climate than instructional effectiveness.

—Charter schools are highly alert to the need to maintain reputations as good places for teachers to work, and though not all have created positive images and supportive working environments, those that have not are prone to failure.

—Though charter schools are aware of the need to maintain relationships with donors, lenders, and providers of assistance, these relationships seldom dominate the attention of school leaders.

—Charter schools are responsive to their authorizers, though school-authorizer relationships are seldom focused solely on the charter and only occasionally turn on issues of the school's academic performance.

Internal Accountability

Internal accountability is the mark of an organization that efficiently uses all its human and financial resources toward a goal. Any organization that must produce something real must have internal accountability. It is especially important for organizations such as schools, where people play specialized roles and the product—student learning—is not created by one person acting alone but by many people acting in combination.

Fred M. Newmann, Bruce M. King, and Mark Rigdon introduced the idea of internal accountability to education.[1] In a school, internal accountability is the set of processes whereby teachers apply shared expectations to their own work and to that of their colleagues. Creating a shared vision of the organization's mission and methods, and maintaining it over time, is the core management function in a professional organization.

In their seminal article, Newmann and his colleagues concluded that external accountability—the demands and expectations of school boards and other external constituencies—can be incompatible with internal accountability.[2] That might be the case for conventional public schools that must respond to monthly changes in school board policy, are subject to abrupt changes in staffing and leadership, and can survive whether or not they satisfy parents and demonstrate growth in student learning. One can readily see how these circumstances would convince teachers and administrators in regular public schools that there is no point working to improve the school as a whole. Even the most dedicated professionals would understandably focus on their own work and leave the rest of the school to take care of itself. But it is not the case with charter schools. External accountability, to authorizers that set definite expectations for performance and to parents, potential teachers, and other supporters, motivates internal accountability.

The charter school movement challenges the theory of loose coupling in education.[3] By making schools' existence dependent on their ability to demonstrate performance, chartering can reward effective combined action and punish unproductive fragmentation.[4] In theory, charter schools, free to improve their methods and forced to maintain their authorizers' support and attract parents, will work hard to say what teachers will do and what students will learn. Also in theory, charter schools will try to create attractive jobs for teachers and try to recruit teachers who will be happy and productive in the roles available. Moreover, charter schools that cannot come together in these ways will, in theory, be forced by their authorizers and other constituencies either to change or to close their doors.

Developing Internal Accountability

Though our case studies identified many charter schools that are rapidly developing mechanisms of internal accountability, few had high degrees of internal accountability from the start. The process of writing a charter application does not necessarily prepare a group to run the kind of school its proposal envisions. Some charter schools were founded on the ideals of individual teacher autonomy and boundary-less exploration that have made many public schools so difficult to integrate. Some charter schools were started by visionaries and rhetoricians who could write proposals and gather groups of enthusiastic individuals but could not lead or manage an organization on a day-to-day basis.

The demands of operating a charter school soon create pressures for purposive, coordinated work. Members of the groups that founded schools were often surprised at one another's actions and were troubled when new teachers just did not seem to get it. Some school founders became disillusioned about how poorly others understood their vision, and some groups of teachers concluded that school heads were causing a great deal of confusion. Parents who came to the school with unspoken expectations that the school had not anticipated quickly became unhappy customers. How schools respond to these initial confusions and disappointments determines whether they will build healthy internal accountability or never get there at all.

With respect to internal accountability, not all schools start at the same place. Schools run by newly formed groups had more trouble than schools sponsored by established organizations, especially those that had prior experience running schools or offering instructional programs. Conventional public schools that sought charter status brought with them old norms of mutual noninterference, and these proved difficult to change. Charter schools with founders who agreed only that they disliked the conventional public school system, or who shared few specific ideas about instruction, experienced great difficulty. So did schools that formed solely on the basis of high-sounding principles (for example, inclusiveness or creativity). Meanwhile, many private schools that applied for charters had already created internal accountability.

Chartering naturally creates three pressures that favor schools with strong internal collaboration and trouble for those that cannot develop it. First, responsible authorizing agencies demand to know whether schools are operating as promised and producing positive student results. Second, parents choose a charter school because they think it is set up to educate their children in ways they find legitimate. Once children start attending school, not all parents are pleased with what they see. Although few parents pull their children out of charter schools, many insist that the schools keep their promises. Third, teachers and administrators accept positions at a charter school on the basis of some understanding of goals and conditions of professional work. They, too, have strong incentives to take action when the school is not operating as promised.

Though many authorizers do not take their responsibilities seriously, some do. Those authorizers that make a serious monitoring effort can readily tell when a school is floundering. In general, schools that do not present and fulfill clear promises to parents about climate and instructional program, that do not present themselves clearly to potential staff and live by their promises, or that look shaky to their authorizers are in for serious problems.

Chartering not only encourages schools to develop internal accountability, but it also usually enables internal accountability by giving schools control of staffing decisions, thus allowing them to hire people who will fit within a coherent conception of a school. In addition, by giving schools control of funds, chartering encourages schools to buy forms of advice and assistance that help professionals converge on a vision of a school's mission and approach to instruction.

Chartering also exempts schools from district-imposed turnover of teaching staff and administrators. Charter schools have staff turnover, too, but it is usually caused by the school's effort to sharpen its self-definition or by an individual's search for a different environment.

Charter schools have an immense advantage over regular public schools. Their relations with authorizers, parents, and potential teachers make it clear that they are enterprises whose value must be apparent to others who have alternatives. Charter schools are not accountable to abstractly defined principles of professionalism or to an amorphous general public. They must act in ways that build and maintain the confidence of particular constituencies. Although good public relations can help schools meet these challenges, charter schools' experience shows that no substitute exists for clarity, coherence, and performance.

An internally accountable school is one in which earnest collaboration is forged on behalf of student learning, based on shared commitments about goals and methods. It is not enough to have high goals absent clear methods or to be committed to using particular methods absent specific plans of action for putting them into practice. Nor, finally, is it enough to use a method of instruction without being prepared to identify instances in which it does not work and to adapt accordingly.

In the newly created charter schools we visited, a pattern of development is apparent. Boards, staffs, and parents pass through periods of turbulence to develop shared expectations about goals and measures of overall performance. In the course of about three years, most schools regularize internal relationships and establish divisions of labor and the basis on which individuals hold one another accountable.[5] Charter schools that survive initial confusions about goals and roles usually develop into organizations very unlike conventional public schools: They are clearer, simpler, less conflict-ridden, and more focused on instruction. Some schools do not survive those confusions.

Difficulty in Developing Internal Accountability

A relatively small minority of charter schools—one in five of those we visited—has been very slow to develop internal accountability. Some schools will never overcome the expectation that someone on the outside (for example, a school board or district central office) will intervene to solve their problems. Few of these survive, though some are still in existence.

Other schools never truly encounter the pressures from parents, teachers, a board, or an authorizing agency that lead to internal accountability. In particular, conversion schools (conventional public schools that, in some states, can choose to adopt charter status) often have great difficulty breaking out of the mold in which they were first made. Because they already have incumbent teaching staffs, school buildings, and neighborhood attendance patterns, many conversion schools do not become accountable to parents and teachers in all the ways that new charters do. Most remain accountable only to the district central office and do not expect their performance to be any more closely monitored after chartering than before. As a result, many conversion schools operate, are staffed, and feel like district-run magnet or theme schools, not like new charters.

These findings from our case studies are reinforced by the national survey data. As figure 3-1 shows, public conversion schools are less likely to report having control of their budgets and what they buy, how they pursue their educational vision through selecting curriculum and hiring teachers, and how they operate and use time.

There are exceptions among conversion charters, for example, the Vaughn Street School in Los Angeles. There, the staff insisted on becoming a school of choice and taking control of the entire per-pupil funding available in the Los Angeles public schools. This created new bases of accountability and new opportunities for change. School head Yvonne Chan, previously a maverick principal within the public school system, also took care to demonstrate that the school had taken advantage of

Figure 3-1. *Control Over Critical Resources and Decisions*

Percent

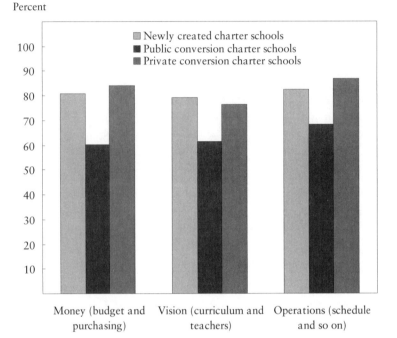

chartering to change instruction, staffing, relations with parents, and use of funds.

Vaughn Street is surely not the only conversion school that now looks more like a new charter than a conventional public school. But many conversion schools regard chartering as an opportunity to make only a few marginal changes. Their leaders take care not to rock the boat, either by challenging district control or by differentiating themselves sharply from other conventional public schools. One California conversion charter, for example, discouraged parents from outside its former attendance zone from enrolling children in the school, to avoid any tension with the school district. Another conversion middle school in California lost control of its size and therefore its instructional program, as district decisions forced it to grow from eight hundred students to fifteen hundred students. The district needed to find places for a growing student population and did not want to create new schools. The school, as a district-sponsored conversion, felt it had no choice but to accept them.

At some conversion schools, parents, and sometimes even school staff, are not aware of how charter status makes the school different. Administrators at one school we visited said it had taken them three years to start a concerted effort to let parents know how their school was different and why it would be important to remain a charter. They realized these parents were otherwise not going to be strong allies if the school's charter status ever came into question.

But while conversion schools can have some difficulty developing internal accountability, they also have some advantages. Schools that convert to charter status avoid some of the start-up crises that afflict new "from scratch" charter schools. As one principal of a conversion school explained, she saw value in the close ties to the school district: District support allowed the staff to concentrate on instructional improvement and avoid the facilities and finance issues that so often plague new schools.

Governing Boards and Internal Accountability

School-level governing boards can play important roles in internal accountability. Most new charter schools have had to form internal governing boards, similar to those that run independent schools. In most states these boards are the legal persons responsible for the school. They also officially undertake financial obligations for the school and are the employers of teachers and administrators. Creating these new boards, which are in effect the official internal oversight mechanisms for the schools, and establishing a productive division of labor between board and staff have proven extremely challenging. But when it works well, an independent board for a public school can promote internal accountability.

As figure 3-2 shows, principals in the two kinds of schools that constitute the vast majority of charter schools—new schools and schools from conventional public status—regard their own governing boards as one of the groups to whom they are most accountable.

There is obviously not one right role for a charter school's governing board. But as we learned from our case studies, clear divisions of labor between board and management are crucial. Different boards err on different sides of the line between board micromanagement and a total lack of mission management and constructive oversight.

Independent or Dependent?

All charter schools, both newly created and conversion, must deal with the question of how much autonomy they have. State laws vary in how much freedom schools will have over curricular, staffing, and financial decisions. State laws also differ on whether the charter school is considered a separate legal entity or whether it is legally an arm of the district. Schools that are considered a separate legal entity or have a high degree of freedom from their authorizer can be thought of as independent charter schools. Those that are legally just another district school or are given little autonomy from union contract provisions and district rules and regulations can be thought of as dependent charter schools.

The difference between independent and dependent status is at least as important as the distinction between conversion and newly created schools. Dependent charter schools are much more likely to experience interference from their authorizers, run into trouble attracting staff whose instructional philosophies fit the mission of the schools, have internal governance problems, and establish a clear understanding with parents about how the school is different from traditional public schools.

Independent conversion schools have all the advantages of a conversion school (that is, a history of running an instructional program, access to a building, and so on) without exposure to shifting staff assignment policies and district mandates that can interfere with the school's efforts to create or maintain itself as a cohesive organization.[1] A school we visited in Georgia that operates with a broad waiver from state laws explained that being a conversion school was a distinct advantage in developing a strong academic improvement plan. As the principal put it, "While brand new schools were dealing with contractors and building inspectors during the start-up years, we got to focus on academics."

1. Another study that found greater flexibility increased internal accountability was conducted by WestEd. See Los Angeles County United School District, *The Findings and Implications of Increased Flexibility and Accountability: An Evolution of Charter Schools in Los Angeles Unified School District* (1998).

Unlike the local site councils required by site-based management programs, most governing boards include, but are not dominated by, current parents and teachers. The board of one Michigan charter school we visited included a lawyer, an insurance agency president, the head of a community bank, a friendly member of the city council, the head of a youth service agency, a respected public school principal, and a parent of a child

Figure 3-2. *Accountability to Governing Boards, Parents, and Chartering Agencies*

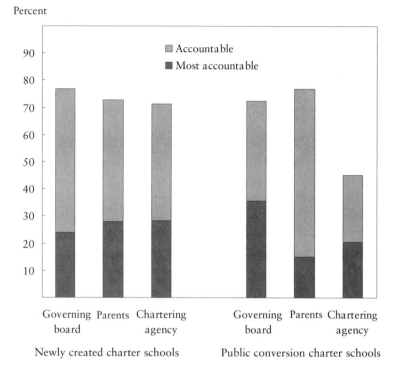

Percent

who had graduated from the school. Boards composed of business people or long-term supporters of the school are inclined to act like business boards; they counsel management on long-term strategy, recruit new school heads, and intervene at times of crisis.

However, many boards of individual schools do not start out with such a disciplined vision of their own role. Boards composed of current parents and teachers often have great difficulty distinguishing their roles from those of management. We heard many stories of parent-teacher or teacher-principal disagreements leading to serious conflicts within such boards as well as to rapid management turnover. At several schools we visited in Arizona, Colorado, and Massachusetts, we learned of boards that went around the school principal and assigned duties directly to the school staff. There were also boards in which factions of current parents pushed for policies that apparently did not reflect the desires of the majority of parents.

School leaders and teachers who come from public schools and other government agencies are not accustomed to working with individual school governing boards. In their experience, district school boards are public representative bodies that have virtually sovereign powers and can regulate or intervene in school operations virtually at will. This view of a board's role is incompatible with a school's internal accountability.

Clarifying relationships between an individual school's governing board and its management is key to the development of internal accountability. Like private sector boards, boards of well-defined charter schools oversee the school's basic identity and strategy but leave day-to-day management to paid professionals. They refer complaints and personnel issues to managers for resolution, and when performance slips to unacceptable levels they look to hire new managers, to whom once again they can entrust day-to-day responsibility.[6] A well-functioning governing board makes the principal and other staff members accountable to a group with nothing at stake other than the interests of the school. Charter school boards should be, in the phrase introduced by David Osborne and Ted Gaebler, the authors of *Reinventing Government*, built to "steer, not row."[7]

Charter Schools' Accountability to Families

Maintaining family confidence is critical to charter school functioning and internal accountability. Schools that cannot attract students do not get funding. Parents want to send their children to schools that provide a caring and motivating climate and effective instruction. Evidence from our interviews confirms the results of national surveys, which show that parents choose charter schools because of the methods of instruction they offer, the safe and studious climate they maintain, and the sense of commitment to the individual child.[8]

To attract parents, charter schools must make, or at least imply, some promises. Most charter schools offer a smaller, more intimate setting, staffed by people who chose to work in the school. Parents also know that charter schools can be more responsive to individual needs than regular public schools, because teachers and staff on site are in charge and cannot dodge a reasonable request by saying "the central office won't let us." Most charter schools also expressly promise to be more open, interesting, focused on academics, and caring than regular public schools.

There are disappointments. Though most parents do not want to continue shopping for schools once they have placed their child in a charter school, all know that they can leave a charter school if it does not keep its promises or if it fails to provide good instruction. Parents do withdraw their children from charter schools.

Some charter schools do not jell quickly. Founder-parents are patient with such schools, but parents who chose such schools expecting them to be fully formed educational institutions can be disappointed. Further, parents are capable of wishful thinking when choosing a charter school. Some believe that a charter school will do things it never promised. Some parents find that methods of instruction that sounded appealing in the abstract do not in fact meet their child's needs. Some who have placed their children in new schools find that the school develops in directions they do not like. Some parents assume that a charter school will accommodate them or their children in any way the family desires, and they find out that it cannot. Others choose charter schools after trying a series of public schools and finding them all somehow wrong for their children. Though a few frequent shopper parents find a charter school to be just right, many are, as Chester E. Finn, Bruno V. Manno, and Gregg Vanourek report, prone to conclude that the charter school is also against them or their children and move on.[9]

Not all parents perceive that they have many choices. For some a charter school is a last resort. For others who have given up on conventional public schools, there is no practical alternative to staying with a charter school that is struggling or has a philosophy with which the parents are not entirely comfortable. When parents see no good options, they are not apt to leave a school unless it becomes emotionally upsetting to their children.

The numbers of parents who remove their children for these reasons are small. But all schools suffer some parent attrition, which creates leverage for new parents and parents who remain. Even the charter schools that have waiting lists understand that they cannot survive if parents lose confidence in them.

In many schools, parents have less to say about day-to-day decisions than many expected they would have. Though parents play significant volunteer and assistance roles in schools founded by parents, few govern. Many schools have difficulty getting parents to attend meetings, even when important decisions are to be made.

For most parents, choosing a charter school is their most important form of involvement. Choice gives parents standing to make reasonable requests. Promises made to parents give teachers and administrators reason to act.

Do charter school leaders understand parents' aspirations and make sure their schools fulfill them? As our analysis of RPP International's national survey of charter school principals shows, charter school leaders think much about what parents want for their children and try to deliver it.[10] For all types of charter schools (new, converted public, and former private), principals think parents most want schools that are small, effective, and adaptive to the needs of students with special talents or disabilities (see figure 3-3).[11]

School leaders are learning how important it is to help form parent expectations before children enroll and to discourage parents who could never be satisfied with the school. One school in Michigan has taken the parent education process especially seriously. When parents (or teachers) approach the director about the school, he or she suggests they purchase books written about the curriculum and philosophy of the school so they have a better understanding of its principles. Staff also hold seminars for existing and potential parents about the school programs and methods. A new district-sponsored school in the Pacific Northwest required prospective students and parents to complete a challenging questionnaire, which explored a family's willingness to have a child forgo television to do significant amounts of homework and to commit to very high rates of attendance and effort. Such mechanisms ensure that parents clearly understand what the school offers. They are designed as much to help parents conclude that they would not be satisfied with the school as to increase enrollment.

What both schools and parents are learning about charter schools is that choice creates reciprocal accountability. Parents must meet the school's expectations as well as vice versa. This relationship is new, and it is one of the charter school movement's greatest contributions to public education.

Figure 3-3. *Agreement with What Parents Care About*

Percent

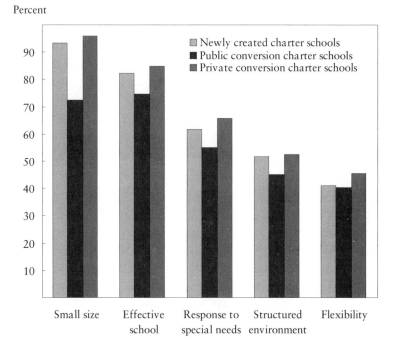

Though critics have warned that schools of choice would cater to parents' every whim, we see no evidence of that. Most charter schools try to attract parents by offering a definite instructional program. Most also promise individualization, but within the boundaries of the school's goals and approach to instruction. Thus a student who needs extra help or some tutoring that provides new angles on the subjects taught can usually get it. But a parent who objects to the school's avowed approach to instruction or who wants special concessions (exemption from attendance and discipline rules or family-supervised homework) is less likely to be accommodated.

In sum, charter schools take account of parents' aspirations, but they are not dominated by parents' demands. Nor do they, as some critics have feared, compete for students on the basis of easy courses, lax requirements, or emphasis on entertaining noncurricular activities. To the contrary, the vast majority of charter schools work to ensure a safe, caring environment. Many also promise high standards and heavy workloads.

These promises are especially attractive to low-income and minority parents who feel that the public schools in their neighborhoods are chaotic and academically inferior.

Charter Schools' Accountability to Teachers

A charter school needs to attract and keep a teaching staff that is both able and willing to provide the kind of instruction promised to parents. Thus every school needs to provide the kinds of working conditions, climate, support, and pay that satisfy current teachers and impress potential teachers that it is a good place to work. The fact that charter schools choose and employ teachers leads to mutual accountability—schools must keep promises to teachers and teachers must perform effectively in the context of the school.

Some teachers have specific preferences about instructional style and would not choose to teach in a school that required methods that made them uncomfortable. Most teachers, however, make more general demands. They want to work in a caring, collegial environment where they carry few administrative burdens and where classroom practice is not always changed by mandates from on high.

School leaders also feel accountable to their teachers. Most of the charter schools we studied regard good teachers as assets that must be cherished and protected. Some schools have strict discipline policies for students and temporarily remove children from a class if they act up. For some teachers, this is an area that makes their job much easier and more rewarding. It also gives them a sense that the administration is there to back them up.

In our case studies we encountered no charter schools that have created exploitative conditions for teachers. Most try to make teaching in the school as rewarding as possible. Because charter schools receive less public money than regular public schools, some offer lower average teacher salaries, though most pay about the same as neighboring public schools for beginning teachers.[12] They try to overcome these disadvantages with pleasant working conditions, careful consultation about important decisions, and more overt appreciation for teacher accomplishments. As Julia E. Koppich,

Patricia Holmes, and Margaret L. Plecki report, most, though not all, charter school teachers say they would choose to teach in a charter school if they had to do it over again.[13]

Some teachers joined charters expecting to play major roles in school governance. There are teacher-run charter schools and a larger number of schools in which a small group of teacher-founders share administrative responsibilities. But most teachers who hoped to decide all matters by committee eventually change their minds. Some see that constant committee work takes too much time away from teaching and gets too little done, and others simply burn out and return to conventional public schools. Most new charter schools settle down rapidly, creating a clear set of well-defined roles, including division of some administrative responsibilities among teachers.

Most teachers who choose to work in charter schools want to collaborate with other teachers, making sure students' knowledge accumulates across different courses and between grade levels. They want school leaders to make collaboration possible by creating free periods for discussion, and they want collaboration rewarded. But as charter schools mature, and teachers come to understand what is possible within them, teachers value internal clarity over open-ended deliberation on all matters.

Even in localities such as Mesa, Arizona, where teachers are scarce and competition between charters and conventional public schools is intense, few charter schools have had trouble attracting capable teaching staffs.[14] Most teachers who choose to join charter schools in their first few years of existence did so because they liked their school's educational philosophy and for other reasons consistent with the development of coherent, productive instructional environments.[15]

Many new charter schools also employ retired public school teachers, who are eligible for pensions and no longer want to work in conventional public schools. If a national teacher shortage predicted for the early 2000s occurs, charter schools might have to recruit high proportions of their teachers from unconventional sources—retired teachers, other retirees, and educated adults who are skilled in other fields but lack teaching experience. Teachers from these sources have had other professional opportunities, and most expect to be treated as if they had real expertise and to be consulted on matters that affect them.

Conversion schools, which often start out with the same teaching staff they had when they were conventional public schools, are highly accountable to teachers. Teachers voted for the conversion, and most negotiated strong roles in internal governance. They also know that the school is in control of its policies, and they can no longer be mollified by claims that the central office requires policies that the teachers do not like. School leaders also know that valuable teachers can choose to leave and that retirement and residential moves will inevitably create turnover. Thus a conversion school's reputation among teachers is extremely important.

Some conversion schools are still required to hire from district teacher pools. Schools that have a definite mission or philosophy and provide clear signals to potential applicants experience little difficulty finding teachers that fit. Meanwhile, conversion schools whose teachers are simply assigned by the school district often have difficulty establishing clear signals about mission and intent. Conversion charter schools whose principals can be abruptly reassigned by the school district experience many problems. They have difficulty promising teachers anything in particular, and accountability to teachers is thus weakened.

As with parents, charter schools' relationships with teachers are not always idyllic. Some charter schools that started out without clear ideas about instruction experienced conflicts within the teaching staff and between school leaders and teachers.[16] New schools that experienced teacher and administrator turnover in their early months either failed or came close to failing. Schools that survived learned to present themselves more clearly to prospective teachers.

A Georgia charter school illustrates the development of a professional environment of shared responsibility and demanding mutual accountability. Teachers report that the school's charter status forced them to work constantly on school improvement. Though teachers started by working in their own autonomous zones, they soon realized that the school was going to be held accountable at the end of the year for test scores, and this led them to begin to talk seriously with each other. Charter school status meant that the school had flexible funds, which allowed it to bring in a consultant who helped the staff focus their development on particular instructional improvement goals.

Many teachers in new schools found the requirement to renew their contracts each year unnerving, but they were convinced of its value. One teacher said that during her four years at a traditional public middle school, no teachers left, even though several were vocally unhappy with their jobs and vigorously resisted efforts to upgrade the school's teaching methods. As this teacher said, turnover can be healthy when it happens for the right reasons. In schools with one-year renewable teacher contracts, good performance is praised, bad performance is dealt with, and people who do not want to work in a common enterprise are encouraged to find other schools where they will fit in better. Teachers we interviewed said this gives the school an atmosphere of fairness and energy.

Authorizers and Internal Accountability

No matter how carefully they manage connections with parents, teachers, and others, charter schools must always tend their relationships with authorizers. Authorizers approve charter applications, release public funds so that schools can use them, and must ultimately decide whether to renew the charter when the school's term expires (five years in most states, up to fifteen years in Arizona, and an unlimited number of years in the District of Columbia and Michigan).[17]

Although authorizers do not control charter schools in detail, their relations with charter schools are critical in certain circumstances. Gaining initial approval, periodic oversight, resolution of complaints against the school, and charter renewal are times when charter schools must persuade authorizers that they are operating as promised and providing good instruction.

Most school leaders remain aware of promises to their authorizer and of unresolved issues that might lead the authorizer to ask for data or conduct a monitoring visit. However, many school leaders know that the authorizer is very unlikely to initiate any contact. This is especially true in states such as Arizona where some authorizers are responsible for dozens of schools but have little or no staff capacity and in states where school districts authorize schools but manifestly take no interest in them.[18]

In general, the more a school is in control of its internal accountability, the less it has to do with its authorizer on a day-to-day basis. School heads, teachers, and parents soon learn that the school is weakened by internal conflicts that draw the attention of authorizers or newspapers. Most school leaders learn to minimize conflicts by describing the school up front in ways that discourage people with incompatible expectations from taking jobs or placing students there.

The ability to handle problems internally is almost certainly a sign of organizational strength and a source of internal accountability. People from within the public school culture, who are accustomed to looking to the central office or the teachers union to resolve conflicts and who do not value the school's autonomy, are slower to see the costs of internal conflict than are people with private sector or nonprofit experience. But most charter schools soon become relatively tight-knit and learn how to address their problems internally.

Inevitably, some problems are too serious or persistent to remain within the school. Because authorizers rapidly come under public pressure when one of their schools becomes involved in a public controversy, most have developed some form of crisis management capacity.

Except during and after crises, few schools hear a great deal from their authorizers. The director of a charter school authorized by the Arizona State Board of Education could not recall a visit from the state board, though he had once met with some officials in a downtown office. Their only correspondence was a letter asking him to explain why his students (who had previously dropped out of the traditional school system) performed below the 35th percentile on the Stanford-9, a state-mandated assessment. He wrote back, saying that most of his students came to the school well below grade-level and that an arbitrary cutoff point "doesn't even begin to touch who we are and what we do."[19] The school director asserted that one of his primary responsibilities was to "shield his staff from the outside world, rather than promote outside input that may be inconsistent with our mission and goals."

Dealing with Authorizers on School Effectiveness

All the charter schools in our sample assess their own academic performance and provide required data to their authorizers. The charter schools we studied were quick to create instructional improvement strategies when

Figure 3-4. *Performance Measures Monitored More Than Once a Year*

Percent

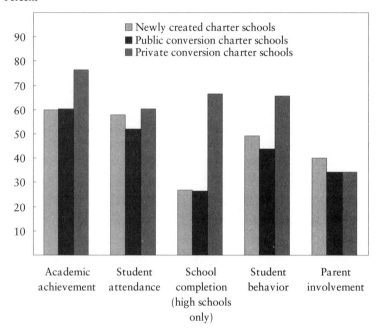

they, their authorizers, or parents identified schoolwide deficiencies in student performance.[20]

Though few authorizers keep detailed track of school outcomes, many schools do. Figure 3-4 shows that most schools track academic performance and student attendance at their own initiative. Many also track other process and outcome measures. In figure 3-4, the difference between schools converted from private versus conventional status is telling. Private schools' habits of self-monitoring and accountability to parents, donors, and so on are far stronger than those of conventional public schools that have converted to charter status. New charters fall between private and public conversion schools.

Local school boards are particularly reluctant to act against charter schools on the basis of student performance, because doing so can expose them to complaints that they have long tolerated similar levels of performance among the conventional public schools they supervise. Nationwide, only four charter schools have been closed by their authorizers for poor academic performance.[21] However, a much larger number, perhaps as many as one in ten charter schools, have received complaints and threats of possible closure based on poor student test results. These interventions almost always lead to intense work within the school (including some brief periods of frantic overwork), leading to greatly increased time on instruction in the areas where the school is weak. In this way charters are no different from conventional public schools that come under threat of sanctions for low performance.[22]

How hard a school works in response to an authorizer's threat depends on whether the authorizer has any real options. One California conversion school received its charter with little trouble. Three years after converting to charter status, however, it was put on a warning list because test scores had fallen. A new school head had just been hired when the test scores came out and was faced with having to explain the drop in scores and prepare the school for its charter renewal, due only a year later. The school reworked its schedule to put greater emphasis on reading and mathematics, and the scores improved, though only enough to get the school off the warning list. The director continued to push for better academic performance, but the staff knew that the school would be hard to close. No other district middle school serving similar demographics performed better than this charter school. Moreover, its fame (national political figures had visited the school and it had created much favorable publicity for the district) and popularity with teachers seemed to secure its place in the district.

All charter school leaders know they must go through renewal some day. Some school leaders think about renewal from the first day the school opens, while others assume nothing need be done until renewal time is near. In many situations, neither the authorizer nor the charter school knows how the renewal process will work; no one knows for sure how schools will be judged or what outcomes will be considered adequate. In these situations, some school leaders hope that they can win renewal simply by trying hard and filling a niche for their students or parents.

Schools in states with multiple authorizers sometimes consider seeking a new charter from another entity, instead of pursuing renewal from the original authorizer. One school in Michigan was unhappy that its authorizer continually imposed new requirements, including more frequent student testing than the state required of all public schools. As the school looked toward the renewal process, it considered switching to another authorizer that had provided support and stable, not growing, regulation for other schools of similar design.

In Arizona, some schools view the state authorizers as bureaucratic and slow, and they have come to favor dealing with school districts. Because a school district can authorize a school any place in the state and can receive a management fee for each school it authorizes, some districts have been willing to authorize many charter schools. Districts differ in their diligence and demands on charter schools, and charter schools can and do shop around to find the type of authorizer relationship they desire.

Conclusions

Chartering puts schools into a unique combination of accountability relationships. These relationships impose many burdens. But do the burdens, and the need to maintain the confidence of multiple constituencies, distract teachers and administrators from the schools' main business of providing effective instruction to students? Based on the available evidence, the answer to that question is a qualified no. For most charter schools, the best way to maintain the confidence of all these constituencies is to tend to the academics, serving students well and keeping promises about the type and quality of instruction delivered. In the vast majority of situations we studied, charter schools do not have to buy off their different constituencies by making concessions that compromise instruction. They can meet their obligations to authorizers, parents, internal board members, teachers, and donors in the same way, by making the school a good place to learn and to teach.

Charter schools do get into trouble. A school threatened with the loss of parents, a teacher walkout, strife on its governing board, or withdrawal of financial support from a donor must go into a crisis mode. Schools that do not resolve these crises perish (or never open, as has happened several times in Chicago and Massachusetts). However, no school in our experience has been twisted permanently out of shape by the actions taken to satisfy one of its main constituencies. To the contrary, schools that survive crises often emerge stronger and better able to serve their students. The continuing pressures from other constituencies can help charter schools regain their balance.

The mechanism by which schools manage their different relationships with external constituencies is internal accountability—a clear division of responsibilities focused on accomplishing the school's goals for students. In charter schools that survive the first three years of turbulence and role clarification, the net effect of the school's relationships with those parties is to strengthen the school's focus on motivating and educating students. Research on private schools can be read in much the same way. It shows that schools can be strengthened by their need to create relationships of trust and confidence with parents, teachers, governing boards, and donors.[23]

CHAPTER FOUR

Authorizing Agencies

Authorizing agencies—typically state and local departments of education, other state agencies, and universities—are key figures in the charter school movement. Their actions can determine whether an individual school will succeed or fail. Authorizers have the sole power to revoke a school's contract and are the government agency primarily responsible for judging the school's academic progress. The relationship between a charter school and its authorizer can enhance or detract from the school's focus on instruction and its internal effectiveness.

At their most basic level, school charters are agreements between authorizing agencies and individual schools about goals, basic modes of operation, and performance requirements. In theory, a well-drafted charter could be the quintessential accountability mechanism. It would establish the authorizing agency's right to expect the school to admit students by known rules and criteria, to serve all students enrolled, and to attain specified student outcomes. The agreement would also establish the school's right to operate without interference, be paid for pupils enrolled, be free to enroll students from a given catchment area, recruit teachers, and have its charter continued or renewed if it meets all specified criteria.

Charter school advocates have long argued that these performance agreements would offer a unique approach to government oversight. They claimed that limiting oversight to the terms of a contract and its performance goals would replace government's focus on compliance to rules and regulations that provide no assurance of whether or not children in a school are learning.

The reality, however, is much different from the theory. Authorizing agencies are having a harder time than anticipated overseeing charter schools. Some, such as universities and state agencies, have never directly overseen schools before and are having to learn how to follow the applicable laws and cope with public scrutiny. Agencies that have traditionally provided public education—local school districts—face an even greater challenge: learning how to oversee public schools on the basis of performance. The challenge district authorizers face is broad. They must find ways to learn how to oversee contracts, not run an organization, and they must find ways to distinguish their oversight of charter schools from their oversight of other public schools. In general, approving agencies are finding they must take the time to invent their own accountability measures and processes from scratch.

Charter authorizing agencies must also define a new kind of relationship with these quasi-independent public schools. Because charter school laws often lack clarity, many gray areas may exist in a school's relationship with a school district authorizer. Is the school part of the district? To what extent does the school administrator have the right to refuse to attend district meetings? Many consider charters as just another form of special or magnet school, still completely controlled by the district.

Because so many approving agencies lack the staff, funding, or time to invest in this process, many approving agencies are reverting back to what is expedient or what they know. More often than not, they judge charter schools on compliance or input measures and excuse poor performance.

This chapter focuses on authorizers and the ways they fulfill their roles. The results of our national survey of charter authorizers and case studies of school-authorizer relationships can be summarized as follows.[1]

—Though many groups were prepared to run charter schools, no government agencies were prepared to oversee them. Authorizers are just beginning to learn how to solicit charter applications; screen applicants to find the most promising providers; and assist, assess the performance of, reward, sanction, terminate, or reauthorize charter schools. Most of these agencies have little organizational capacity to develop the new expertise they need.

—In this environment of uncertainty, charter schools are learning to be proactive and are helping authorizers learn to oversee them effectively.

—Authorizers differ on how willing they are to approve charter applications and how assiduously they monitor the performance of schools they have chartered. Though authorizers' duties and powers vary from state to state, neither state law nor an authorizer's status (as a school district, special-purpose state charter office, or other state entity) is a perfect predictor of how an authorizer will relate to schools.

Our national survey of charter school authorizers classified these agencies into three types: (1) state colleges and universities; (2) local education agencies, mainly local school districts; and (3) state agencies, such as state departments of education or new special-purpose state chartering agencies.

Charter Authorizing Agencies Starting from Scratch

Public school boards and other authorizers are not accustomed to receiving proposals from new groups that want to run schools, subjecting such proposals to careful review, establishing enforceable performance agreements with individual schools, monitoring schools on the basis of performance, or making decisions on whether a school will live or die based on whether the school performs as promised. Moreover, few authorizers are accustomed to overseeing schools that control their own resources, hire staff, and maintain the confidence of parents and teachers, lenders, and private funders. Whether authorizers are school districts, newly created state agencies, or existing state agencies (such as colleges and universities) or city governments that are newly empowered to sponsor charter schools, all must solve unfamiliar problems and develop new capacities.

Most authorizers received their first charter school applications before they had created a specific review and selection process. They created ad hoc processes for the first applications and applied lessons learned from oversights in the first approval processes to later applications. However, because of shifting requirements, lack of clear written policies, and rapid

Figure 4-1. *Authorizers Providing Written Accountability Standards and a Formal Renewal Process*

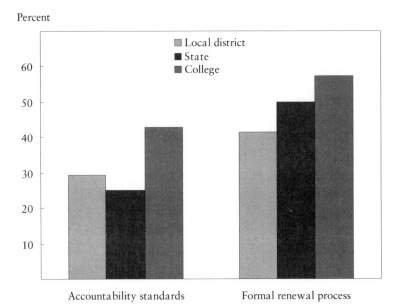

Percent

Accountability standards   Formal renewal process

turnover of central office staff, potential charter applicants in many localities still have reason to wonder what steps they must go through to gain approval and what criteria will be applied by the authorizer, despite several years of experience.

The ad hoc character of authorizers' actions usually continues after school charters are granted. In our survey, only 27 percent of the chartering agencies surveyed reported having written accountability standards, and an additional 4 percent said these were under development. Similarly, only 38 percent of the agencies surveyed had a formal renewal process. Another 6 percent were developing such a process at the time of our survey. As figure 4-1 shows, state colleges and universities that chartered schools are somewhat more likely than other authorizers to provide well-structured accountability processes.

For those agencies with renewal processes in place, the most commonly required reports from schools were formal records of school progress toward goals (cited by 29 percent of all authorizers), a final summary report from the school, and a financial audit. Few agencies require the completion of a renewal application form or a strategic plan for the future of the school.

State charter school laws (and state regulations implementing such laws) generally assume that charter schools will administer student achievement tests and results will be compared with some standard or reference group. It is often the authorizers' job to identify tests and perform the appropriate comparisons. Authorizers also must judge schools fairly, taking account of differences in the schools' missions, neighborhood circumstances, and the prior academic preparation of students served. To support these complex judgments, authorizers not only must obtain quantitative outcomes data such as student test scores and dropout rates, but also must take account of more complex aspects of performance—fulfillment of promises, quality of teaching, and rigor of curriculum.

Many states still have not established the standards to which charter schools will be held at renewal time. Some legislators and state officials argue that as long as the schools are performing adequately, satisfying parents and drawing enough students, they should be allowed to continue. Others say that even if parents are happy with a school, if it is not outperforming conventional schools with similar demographics, it should not be renewed. Even within the same authorizing organization, opinions differ on this subject. Most states have just entered the renewal process for their first round of charter schools. They are learning how to balance the many competing opinions of how charter schools' performance should be measured and valued.

Though only a minority of chartering agencies have written accountability standards or a formal renewal process, most require collection and reporting of some form of student achievement data. As figure 4-2 shows, all state agencies and the vast majority of other authorizers required at least one student achievement test per year.[2]

Regardless of the quality of performance information they receive, most authorizers ultimately judge charter schools in ways that are familiar to government agencies—responding to complaints and reacting to crises. Most authorizers are not, however, well prepared for such events and lack warning or probation routines that would help them to deal with a problem in a school whose overall performance is not poor enough to warrant

Figure 4-2.   *Authorizers Requiring Achievement Tests and Other Data on School Performance*

Percent

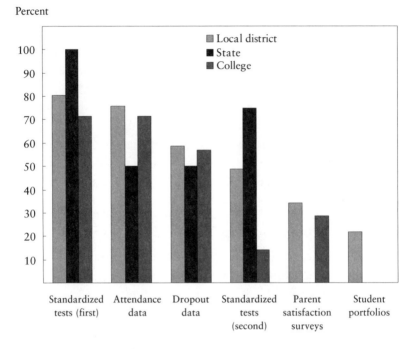

charter cancellation. Local school districts are particularly ill equipped in this regard.

In this light, it is no surprise that just over one-third of all the agencies have ever conducted an investigation of a charter school. As figure 4-3 shows, of all the types of authorizers, state colleges and universities were the most likely to have taken such a step.

Complaints received from parents were the most common trigger for an investigation of a charter school, with 29 percent of the agencies reporting such complaints. Other fairly important triggers were failure to comply with terms of the charter and financial irregularities. A mere handful of agencies reported investigating a charter school because of low test scores, declining enrollment, or complaints from teachers unions.

Despite their announced interest in academic achievement, most authorizers monitor charter schools via financial reports and site visits, not through reports on student achievement. Our analysis of RPP Interna-

Figure 4-3. *Formal Warning System and Investigation Conducted by Local Districts, States, and Colleges and Universities*

Percent

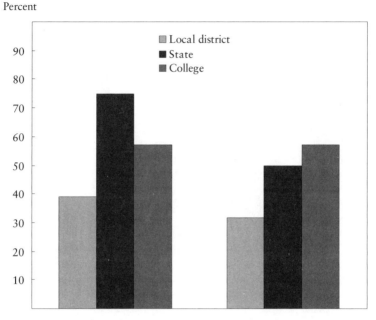

tional's national survey of charter schools shows that schools receive more requests for information on finances than any other topic.[3] Our survey of authorizers confirms this. As figure 4-4 shows, the vast majority of chartering agencies monitors schools via an annual financial report and narrative progress reports. School districts and state colleges and universities also relied on site visits in which agency staff or consultants develop a general impression of the school's health. (Based on our case studies, however, these visits must not be very frequent. Few schools reported being visited by their authorizer more than once each year.)

Most authorizers have limited staff and little experience in a role that requires them to make judgments about school performance that are supposed to lead to life-and-death decisions about individual schools. Authorizers of all kinds (districts and others) are often hamstrung by lack of funding or people power to use tools, even if they had them. Often, they employ one or two people to handle the workload of approving and over-

Figure 4-4. *Methods of Monitoring Performance*

Percent

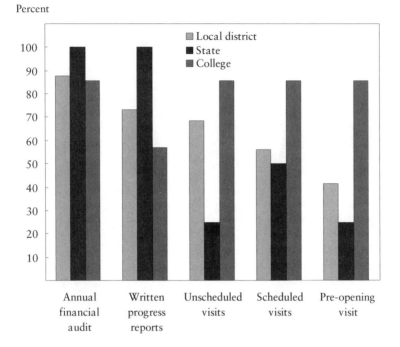

seeing charter schools. In some cases, such as one agency in Arizona, two people oversee more than fifty schools in a wide geographic area. They do not have the manpower to visit their schools, so they invest their time in approving new schools and taking care of any serious problems that arise.

Some agencies can take fees from schools or otherwise get money to support thorough oversight. However, even when they have money, some, such as authorizers in Arizona, come under political pressure to not hire new staff to reduce layers of bureaucracy. Larger agencies, such as the Massachusetts State Board of Education or Central Michigan University (CMU), have turned to contractors to perform oversight functions for them. Smaller districts have usually relied on using current staff in various departments to oversee different aspects of the charter schools' programs.

Charter school leaders in many states have learned that their authorizers lack capacity and might not be able to judge them on the basis of performance. They therefore deal with authorizers politically, building personal relationships and accumulating supporters who might protest any actions negative to the school.

Authorizing agency approaches toward charter schools can be characterized in two ways: whether the authorizer is enthusiastic, reluctant, or ambivalent about authorizing charter schools; or whether an agency commits to cursory oversight, or to compliance-oriented or performance-based oversight, of the charter schools it has authorized.[4] The vast majority of authorizers fit into one of four categories: (1) overeager approvers and inattentive overseers, (2) reluctant authorizers and suspicious auditors, (3) ambivalent approvers and indifferent managers, or (4) professional authorizers and competent stewards.

Overeager Approvers, Inattentive Overseers

A few agencies have approved large numbers of charter schools without making a strong commitment to either assist or oversee schools. Arizona is probably the bellwether state in this regard. Authorizers there believe that by lowering barriers to entry for new schools, they will establish a large number of schools with diverse missions and pedagogy, and they will let competition and parent choice drive quality.

In an effort to get as many independent schools operating as possible, Arizona's legislation created multiple sources for approval so schools could proliferate, provide options for parents, and put pressure on other schools to adapt. To ensure that charter schools would not run into political barriers to approval, Arizona's charter law created a new state entity, the State Board for Charter Schools, whose only mission is to charter schools. The law also gave authority to the state board of education and local school districts that may sponsor schools located outside their district.

Much less attention has been given to how Arizona charter schools would be held accountable by their authorizers. The dominant political figures behind the charter school movement in Arizona believed strongly that parent choice and vigilance would be the most effective accountability measures. Of lesser importance were the application process, start-up and technical assistance, agency oversight, and the charter renewal process. In practice, parent choice has been the major performance accountability mechanism for Arizona's charter schools.

After acting as primary sponsor of the bill, Lisa Graham Keegan was elected state superintendent of public instruction and remained a vocal proponent of charter schools. She and the governor tried to resist onerous new bureaucratic requirements proposed by the Arizona Department of Education. Staffing for the two state boards was kept small. The original application process was easy, requiring little in the way of education or business plans. A combination of a hands-off philosophy toward charter schools and a sheer lack of people power has resulted in Arizona authorizers taking a minimalist approach to monitoring or assisting the schools. They generally leave school survival to depend on two things: the ability of schools to sustain themselves as organizations and parents' willingness to send their children to the school. Most authorizing agencies in Arizona have so far conducted their oversight by responding to parent complaints, especially those related to the legality of charter school practices.

One result is that Arizona leads the country in the number of charter schools, with 348 operating schools in September 1999. Charter schools account for approximately 20 percent of Arizona schools, nearly all of which were sponsored through the two state boards. As the number of schools has grown, both state boards have created increasingly stringent application requirements in an effort to screen out unqualified applicants and have begun to increase their attention to school performance. In 2001 outside organizations such as the Goldwater Institute (a conservative Arizona think tank) and the Arizona Charter Schools Association stepped up their provision of technical assistance to charter schools and are developing voluntary peer review evaluation processes.

Reluctant Authorizers, Suspicious Auditors

These authorizers, who could not be more different from the overeager approvers, are typically local school districts that feel forced by political or legal pressure to sponsor charter schools. They are frequently reluctant to issue charters and eager to find fault with schools operating under a charter. (Conversely, they may deliberately ignore visible problems within a charter school, hoping that the inevitable public nature of the school's problem will tarnish the charter concept.)

These boards often see new charters as someone else's schools that draw funds, students, and teachers away from "their" schools. This can lead to reluctance to transfer funds and a refusal to give new schools access to school district facilities. One indication of the effects of this dislike can be found in the following fact: Of all the local school districts empowered to authorize charter schools in the six states covered by this study, only 7 percent have ever done so.

The scale and type of charter schools authorized are important factors in sponsor-charter relations. Districts may ignore (or even champion) a few small charter schools that do not make a big dent in their budget or that educate difficult-to-serve students. But authorizer attitudes can change when the funds transferred to charter schools force cuts in district staffing or programs. This can happen in small districts with only one or two charter schools or in larger districts (for example, Boston) with six to ten charter schools. In all but the giant districts (for example, Chicago and Los Angeles), ten or more charter schools create critical mass, threaten to develop a strong new political constituency, and force painful changes in district budgets.

Local boards often see charter schools as threatening their own powers, because charters are not always subject to day-to-day changes in school board policies. Many also resent the fact that school boards retain some legal responsibility for charters but do not control them. Local district officials we interviewed throughout the country made statements to the effect that "It is unfair that we are ultimately liable for the actions of charter schools, though we do not control what they do."

Reluctant authorizers normally feel differently about conversion schools, most of which remain closely tied to the district, as they are firmly within the district's control. However, conversion schools maintain smooth relations with their authorizers at some cost. They seldom get the control of staffing, programs, or student recruitment that other charter schools have.

Ambivalent Approvers, Indifferent Managers

Most local school boards that authorize schools fit into this category, as do many state departments of education.

For local public school districts that fit this category, chartering is a minor part of their mission. School districts run large numbers of schools directly, and charters are, with very few exceptions, a minor (and also a new and unfamiliar) part of their portfolio. Similarly, a state department of education may or may not see chartering as a major part of its mission. If not, chartering can easily become an orphan, overshadowed by other and more familiar responsibilities and slighted by staffers who resent any challenge to conventional public education.

Few school districts have created the capability to judge individual schools primarily on the basis of performance, and few want to. A local board faced with unambiguous evidence of a school's failure might have to make extremely painful decisions about school closure, termination of staff, and creation of new options for students. These dynamics are especially evident in California, which has the greatest number of conversion schools (conventional public schools that have petitioned their local boards for charter status), and in Colorado, where many authorizers are local school districts. Local boards typically avoid close monitoring of student performance, preferring to rely on more familiar methods of financial and compliance oversight.

Few of these agencies closely oversee the performance of charter schools. They assume that decisions on charter continuation will ultimately be political (depending on whether a school has maintained parent or foundation support or, conversely, lost credibility because of a scandal), not based on performance. Thus the majority of local school boards have not rigorously overseen, guided, admonished, or closed charter schools.

Many local school boards view charter schools as an outlet for unhappy parents and activists who want to start their own schools. School districts that take these attitudes overlook the distinctive features of charter schools—for example, that they are supposed to have control of their own funds and staff and are supposed to be assessed in terms of performance, not compliance. They try to treat charter schools in familiar terms, regarding them as equivalents to magnet and special schools run by the district itself.

Fast-growing districts in some states have also chartered schools to shift the cost of providing new facilities to charter school operators. Similarly, some state departments of education have sponsored a few schools to avoid criticism from pro-charter legislators. Agencies that charter schools for these reasons are likely to consider their jobs done once the schools are established and will generally leave those schools alone unless they run into financial trouble or become controversial.

In charter schools overseen by ambivalent authorizers, poor student performance is rarely a reason to shut down a school. Few of these authorizers are willing to bother to revoke a charter or fail to renew one, whether or not a school is performing well. Confounding the expectations of charter school advocates, most of these authorizers assume that charter schools, like conventional public schools, will continue indefinitely.

Professional Approvers, Competent Overseers

Most agencies assuming this active role were created specifically for the purpose of chartering schools. Authorizers whose only way to provide schools is through chartering are more likely to think long and hard about approval and monitoring—how to help schools get started, how to oversee school performance, and how to distinguish proposals from groups likely to be able to open and run schools from those likely to fail.

However, local political forces and individual views can be as important as legal status in causing agencies to take this approach. Massachusetts law, for instance, says little about how the state should hold individual charter schools accountable, yet Massachusetts has developed what many consider to be a model accountability system. The Massachusetts Board of Education has taken a slow, controlled approach to authorizing charter schools. As it learned what capacities groups must have to start well-organized schools, the state board imposed increasingly high standards for applicants. It has also visited schools often and created an inspectorate to assess charter school programs in advance of the need to decide on renewal applications. Massachusetts's cautious law and implementation enabled the authorizing agency to focus on school quality by imposing strict limits on the numbers of schools that could be authorized at any one time and by centralizing all authority into one agency that had no other duties.

The Chicago school district, where the mayor, school officials, and business leaders all have put intense effort into ensuring charter school quality, has taken a similarly intense oversight approach to charter school accountability. A few other local school district boards also fit this category. They view charters in a positive light, usually as part of a strategy for introducing high standards and greater performance accountability to the district as a whole—or as a way to replace low-performing schools that have resisted improvement efforts. A small number of districts have come to consider chartering as a promising way to provide schools. Chicago, Illinois, San Carlos, California, Cobb County, Georgia, and Jefferson County, Colorado, all consider charter schools to be one among several ways they can provide schooling options for families. Many more local school districts could operate this way.

Agencies that are committed to charter schools but determined to promote quality try to minimize school problems and failures. They screen applicants well, make sure the schools prepare good instructional plans, and know how to get financial and management help. They set priorities so that chartering is used to provide new options for the neighborhoods or age groups with the weakest public schools. They discover quickly that new schools need help and either find it or create it. These agencies either build significant in-house capabilities or partner with other organizations. In the case of a school district authorizer, this is not just an extension of the district's normal ways of doing business. Chicago quickly realized this and now relies on private actors for financial and governance assessment.

Another authorizer, Central Michigan University, increased the rigor of its approval and monitoring responsibilities only after coming under fire for lax practices. In 1998 a new charter schools' office director created a "little state department" that would make sure all schools chartered by CMU complied with all state requirements. The director is building a staff of sixteen people who will specialize in four functions: governance, finance, instruction, and technical assistance and research. Central Michigan is also thinking about creating a regional structure, with governance, finance, and education staffs in several locations. Because it gains fees from all the schools it charters, CMU can afford to expand its charter schools' office as the numbers of schools increase. The move toward regional offices and attempts to streamline the reporting processes for the schools reflect a concerted attempt by CMU to provide schools with a supportive operating environment.

These four approaches to charter school oversight are not necessarily what policymakers contemplated or hoped for in various state laws, but it is difficult to judge whether any one approach is the most appropriate for all states and communities. There are true benefits and costs to each orientation. The professional approvers are probably most effective in assuring a limited number of academically solid charter schools. However, these agencies may be more bureaucratically oriented than desired by some communities. The overeager approvers are unlikely to develop stringent oversight mechanisms, but they may be more appropriate for states and districts that hope to stimulate district competition and create a marketplace of options for parent choice. Though such a relationship can be difficult for both parties, even reluctant authorizers can serve a useful purpose, as such agencies are often forced to grapple with performance-monitoring issues they might otherwise have chosen to ignore.

Despite these dramatically different approaches to charter school approval and oversight, by making mistakes and sharing lessons learned, all of these agencies are redefining the role of government agencies in overseeing public schools.

Conclusion

Charter schooling is defining a new model for how government can oversee schools on the basis of results instead of politics and rules. But the model is in its infancy. Government agencies are lagging behind schools in understanding what must be done if charter schools are to contribute to public education. Many authorizers are, however, learning about what it takes for a school to succeed and they are increasingly raising the bar for school applicants.

In general, authorizers whose only way to provide schools is through chartering make that their mission. Compared with authorizers for whom chartering is an exception to the normal way they provide schools, these new authorizers are highly concerned about learning to oversee schools— how to distinguish proposals from groups likely to be able to open and run schools from those likely to fail, how to help schools get started, and how to oversee school performance. Many of these agency heads are people with political as well as managerial credibility. They act to build a new agency's track record and preserve their own personal reputations. Authorizers committed to chartering think of an unfilled slot for a charter school as a scarce resource, and they are unwilling to risk it on a school that looks like a long shot.

The authorizers we studied have accumulated only five years' experience with charter schools. Most authorizers have sponsored fewer than five charter schools and have closed none. When asked what changes they would make given their experience, most authorizers emphasized clarifying expectations and increasing monitoring of charter school operations and outcomes. In one way or another, most agency heads echoed one who wrote in our survey that the agency would give "stronger emphasis on performance objectives, performance criteria, benchmarks and measurement." Such desire for better-structured measurement and oversight is surely evidence that at least some authorizers are coming, however slowly, to understand their responsibilities for assessing the performance of the charter and noncharter schools they oversee.

CHAPTER FIVE

Accountability
to Others

Because of their unique level of freedom to partner with nonprofit organizations and to hire outside vendors, and because they are generally left to their own devices to find and finance their own buildings and administer their own funds, charter schools establish voluntary relationships with a set of actors not normally a part of the public school accountability equation. Charter schools depend on these new actors to varying degrees. Charter schools that have close ties to a sponsoring school district, for instance, tend to rely less on independent actors, as the district provides the majority of their services.

And because of their unique level of autonomy and their controversial political status, charter schools also often have many nondiscretionary accountability relationships with political interest groups and with government agencies other than their authorizers. These relationships can impose burdens not anticipated either by the legislators who sponsored state charter laws or by groups that operate charter schools.

In our case studies of charter schools, we approached the question of accountability to these independent actors hoping to learn how these new relationships have affected the school's priorities and performance, and in particular whether they distracted from, or reinforced the school's focus on, instructional quality and student performance. We have found the following:

—Charter schools are more dependent on outside entities than are traditional schools. While district-run schools can get help from the central office, charter schools generally have no option but to build relationships with donors and independent organizations.

—While there are clearly both advantages and risks to this reliance, such voluntary and reciprocal relationships can strengthen the school's academic performance and its internal accountability if the school has strong leadership.

—However, involuntary and one-way relationships with outside entities, especially government enforcement agencies whose role vis-à-vis charter schools has never been clearly defined, can seriously threaten a school's ability to focus on teaching and learning. Pressures from regulatory agencies can eclipse a charter school's relationships with parents, teachers, and even with its authorizing agency.

Voluntary Associations

Unlike traditional public schools, which depend on their local school district central offices for virtually everything—funding, staff, facilities, teacher training, equipment, supplies, building repairs, janitorial service, and so on—charter schools must obtain many essential goods and services for themselves. Education management companies (such as Edison Schools) and outside funders normally work directly with charter schools. These voluntary relationships create mutual benefit and dependency between charter schools and many other entities that heretofore played little or no role in public education.[1] These relationships vary in their intensity and in their impact on the school's financial or academic operations. But in their strongest forms, they can have a powerful effect on a school's priorities and actions.

Many such providers have real influence on charter schools. They include donors, lenders, contractors, charter school associations, and evaluators. Many of them can play positive roles in promoting schools' internal accountability. For example, lenders, including groups set up to advance money to charter schools and other social service organizations, often demand clarification of charter schools' governance structures and require higher accounting standards than charter schools might otherwise follow. Other providers may have philanthropic motives and care less about administrative standards than about good educational performance. However, such providers, including private individuals who may donate legal or management services, can become discouraged if a charter school appears conflict-ridden, chaotic, or ineffective.

Some of these relationships can influence the school's internal operations and therefore indirectly promote strong internal accountability. Others can more directly offer stronger checks and balances to ensure that the school is financially, organizationally, and educationally viable.

Charter Schools' Key Voluntary Relationships

Charter schools' key internal and external voluntary relationships are with donors, lenders, contractors, associations, and evaluators. Donors on which charter schools depend and are thus in some ways accountable include partner organizations, organizations that provide space and facilities, groups that donate goods and services, and sources of private or government grants.

PARTNER ORGANIZATIONS. Community nonprofit organizations such as youth centers, YMCAs (Young Men's Christian Associations), museums, and so on can make charter schools one of their programs.

Many of these organizations are nonprofit human service providers that have been around for a while, have a good reputation for the social service work they do, and see a connection between running a school and providing some kind of social service. Their reputations make them attractive candidates for running charter schools.

Some such organizations may assist the school, not take legal responsibility for it. But their association with the charter proposal is often a selling point for the authorizer as well as for parents. The agendas of these organizations influence what schools become. Their organizations' administrative and financial strengths also help schools do things that freestanding new charters have a hard time doing, such as obtaining grants and bank loans.

ORGANIZATIONS THAT PROVIDE SPACE AND FACILITIES. Organizations providing space and facilities for charter schools can establish a simple landlord-tenant relationship. Sometimes the landlord can be a de facto sponsor, providing space at reduced cost or free. One school we visited is developing a facilities partnership with a state university. The university will provide land to the school, and the school will construct and own its own building. The university as a result has a stake in the school's reputation and its financial viability.

GROUPS THAT DONATE GOODS AND SERVICES. Local businesses, church groups, and other entities often donate supplies and services to charter schools. These may be temporary relationships, and the total resources donated may not be large, but the sense of obligation may be significant. Charter schools tend to rely more on volunteer goods and services than do traditional public schools.

These relationships could be very important if the donations are continuing or are subject to termination (that is, if the school is in donated space and might be evicted, or if a clinic provides a nurse but might withdraw him or her).

SOURCES OF PRIVATE OR GOVERNMENT GRANTS. Grant funding is a significant source of income for many charter schools. In Massachusetts, for instance, charter schools depend on private grants or donations for as much as 37 percent of their operating budgets, whereas public schools often receive no grant funds.[2] These private sources use some judgment in deciding whether to fund a school initially and whether to continue that funding. Charter schools we interviewed regarded private funding sources as involving less paperwork but just as much, if not more, accountability for promised results.

Grants, especially from government agencies, also sometimes impose judgment on schools and are competitive. However, some schools, charter or others, purposefully stay away from government grants (such as Title I) for which they would be entitled, because they eschew more government involvement than they already have and want to avoid any more paperwork hassles. Their goal is to stay as autonomous as possible.

Charter schools also depend upon (and thus become in some ways accountable to) lenders, especially banks and bonding authorities. More and more charter schools are borrowing funds for capital expenses and other high costs. Banks and other sources of such funding are becoming increasingly open to the idea of lending to charter schools. While these organizations are not primarily concerned with the school's academic progress, those who lend money to a school want to see evidence that the school's leadership, governance structures, and relations with its sponsor are stable. A charter school in Colorado, for example, recently received a BBB rating for bonding because of its stability.[3]

Charter schools also enter contracts for assistance. They thus depend on the performance of these contractors and are also in some ways accountable to them. Assistance contractors include school design organizations that manage instructional programs, providers of legal advice and insurance, service providers, and charter school associations and technical assistance organizations.

SCHOOL DESIGN ORGANIZATIONS THAT MANAGE INSTRUCTIONAL PROGRAMS.   A growing number of charter schools contract with vendors (for example, SABIS International, Edison Schools, Beacon Management Services, National Heritage Academies). As managers of the school's instructional program, they influence or directly control hiring, instructional plans, budgets, self-assessment, and relationships with parents. Because some charters specify a relationship with a particular contractor, the school's board can find it difficult (though not impossible) to abandon such an arrangement. In turn, these companies have obligations to their administration and investors, creating several levels of interdependency that may or may not conflict.

PROVIDERS OF LEGAL ADVICE AND INSURANCE.   Providers of legal advice and insurance influence what schools can do and what risks they must eliminate. These actors do not hold any direct power over the school, but they are important in that they can help the school understand and comply with its legal duties. Traditional public schools are not typically distinct legal entities, and thus legal and insurance issues are normally managed at the district level.

SERVICE PROVIDERS.   Schools and their sponsors are increasingly hiring outside contractors to provide services that districts typically offer. These range from accounting services to inspectors who assess the school's educational progress. Such third-party arrangements can introduce a new level of objectivity into the typical school-district relationship and therefore change the nature of how school accountability functions.

Some schools use private organizations for financial management, but because they focus strictly on accounting, few have tried to influence the instructional practices of their client schools.

CHARTER SCHOOL ASSOCIATIONS AND TECHNICAL ASSISTANCE ORGANIZATIONS.   In most states, charter schools can turn to charter school associations or technical assistance organizations for advice and support. These are voluntary associations, but because they help schools learn from one another's experiences with authorizers and unions, they create mutual dependencies. Often, charter schools see their reputations bound to other charter schools in the state or community, leading to a desire to help other schools succeed.[4] As a result, some associations are creating self-assessment and accountability models that will influence schools' relationships with their authorizers. These organizations also frequently influence state laws and rulemaking, so schools both depend on them and need to influence them.

Charter schools are evaluated by independent organizations, which may or may not have any connection with the government agencies that oversee the schools. These include accreditation agencies, researchers, and school design networks.

ACCREDITATION AGENCIES.   Many states require or encourage schools to receive accreditation from an established group such as the North Central Association of Colleges and Schools. Schools often seek accreditation on their own because it allows their students to transfer credit more easily between schools and is more easily understood by colleges and universities. These accreditation bodies vary in the ways they judge schools. Some are much more input-oriented than others, in that they look to see whether schools are offering required courses instead of trying to assess how well a school is teaching its courses. These agencies or the individuals who visit the schools often have particular ideas about good instruction, which may not mesh with the school's philosophy. In some cases, these organizations provide a valued outside perspective on the school's educational program. Thus accreditation agencies can play an important role in helping or hindering schools' internal accountability as well as serve as an intermediary source of judgment for authorizing agencies.

RESEARCHERS.   Every charter school we visited hosts researchers on a regular basis. The principals, teachers, students, parents, governing board members, and others at these schools are interviewed by analysts working on state, federal, and independent projects; by graduate and high school students; and by researchers from other countries. One school we visited hosted more than one hundred visitors in 1999 alone. Not all of these researchers intend to pass any judgment on the school. Many are simply there to get ideas or amass information. But some visits are very high-stakes evaluations. A negative portrayal in a public report threatens a school's future enrollment and may affect a school's relationship with its sponsor. Some schools use researchers to validate their efforts, build support elsewhere, countervail critics, and buttress themselves against members of the authorization agency who do not like them.

SCHOOL DESIGN NETWORKS.   Groups of schools using similar approaches to instruction often come to depend on one another. Informal networks are those encouraged by school design organizations such as New American Schools and the Coalition of Essential Schools. These networks can set expectations for schools to go beyond the requirements of their government authorizers in developing and using good indicators of success. With increasing pressure for school design networks to prove their effectiveness, this trend should be a positive force for encouraging schools' internal and external accountability. Voluntary networks can offer assistance and encouragement for self-assessment and school improvement without making the threat of charter cancellation that is always implicit in a school's relationship with its authorizer.

How Accountability Relationships Affect Schools

Outside organizations can play a significant role in the lives of charter schools, particularly in new schools and schools authorized by entities other than local school boards. (Conversion schools and schools authorized by school boards usually have close legal ties to districts and are not discrete legal entities.) We tried to assess the effects of these relationships: How have they influenced instruction, resource allocation, or student selection in ways that might have a positive or negative effect on school quality or equity?

Accountability to outside organizations is one of the more controversial elements of the new accountability arrangements under which charter schools operate. The public and politicians often fear that by opening schools up to diverse interests, especially those with profit motives, schools will be less focused on the public interest of improved student learning and high-quality instruction. Amy Stuart Wells and Janelle Scott argue that an inherent inequity is built into charter schooling because governing bodies vary in their ability to monitor the performance of contractors.[5] They maintain that this puts charter schools in low-income districts at a disadvantage because local boards in those districts are least able to oversee them effectively. In a recent statement, the executive vice president of the American Federation of Teachers raised concerns about school choice models that transfer authority away from the government and locally elected school boards and give that authority to groups that are not accountable to the people.[6]

As we learned from our case studies, charter schools' dependence on outside organizations has both positive and negative aspects. Whether the effect is primarily positive or negative is largely determined by the strength of the school's governing board—how seriously it takes its role, how sophisticated its members are, how the management company's contract is structured, and so on.

We saw no evidence to suggest that, on the whole, encouraging schools to form outside relationships necessarily detracts from the quality of instruction provided or the ability of faculty and staff to concentrate their attention on teaching and learning. In fact, we saw several instances in which outside organizations had a beneficial effect on a school's performance and internal accountability.

While we have seen variation in schools' capacity to manage contractors, we did not find that the ability to manage contracts had any relationship to the types of populations served by the school or the school's per-pupil operating revenues. Variation in capacity is a real issue. However, the capacity of the school leadership and governing board stems not from the socioeconomic status of the students served but from the prior experience and contacts of members of the governing board. We visited some very low income schools whose governing boards were carefully composed to provide legal and political expertise and access to foundations and other community resources. Approving agencies can encourage the formation of competent governing boards by creating rigorous approval processes and intervening in schools that are failing as a result of poor management. Technical assistance organizations and charter school associations can also play critical roles by helping school founders understand the importance of a strong governing board and by helping board members understand the trade-offs involved in contracting with for-profit providers.

POTENTIAL POSITIVE EFFECTS OF VOLUNTARY ASSOCIATIONS. Charter schools' dependence on outside actors can have a beneficial effect on schools' efforts to develop strong internal accountability. Donors and sources of assistance can help a school increase its capacity to provide good instruction; they can also become sources of constructive pressure for continuous improvement. Depending on the circumstances of an individual school, accountability to donors and sources of assistance can strengthen forces for performance and organizational viability more than a school's relationships with its authorizer; provide critical expertise and access to resources; provide political connections that buffer the school from attacks that would otherwise dominate staff time and attention and weaken their focus on instruction; and increase schools' access to facilities, and develop innovative ways of housing charter schools.

Strengthening Forces for Performance and Organizational Viability. Authorizing agencies often play an insignificant role in prodding schools to work toward academic improvement. Much more powerful influences are those closest to the school's governing board.

One school we visited is funded in part by two well-known organizations (one for-profit, one nonprofit), and the representatives of those organizations sit on the school's governing board. Because these organizations' reputations are intimately tied to the school, school leaders feel constant, strong pressure to maintain the school's image as an excellent place for children to learn. Partners care about their own reputations and feel the school's performance reflects on them. In contrast, the school's authorizing agency seems much less concerned with the school's performance, and parents at the school are interested mainly in their own child's performance, not that of the school as a whole.

For-profit management companies are closely scrutinized by researchers and skeptics, so they have an extra incentive to demonstrate their value to schools. It was beyond the scope of our study to assess the effectiveness of for-profit education management companies, but in our sample, the schools we visited that were managed by education management organizations (EMOs) had some of the clearer accountability agreements and tended to be more willing than most charter schools to be judged on standardized test scores.

A school we visited in Arizona says that its accountability is validated via a regional certification group. Their charter authorizer is little more than an annoyance and certainly does not appear to be adequately monitoring the school's progress or prodding the faculty to improve their practice. When asked if he could do as good a job, or better, if he were left alone, the director responded, "I believe so, we have an internal motivation to validate what we do against external standards."

Providing Critical Expertise and Access to Resources. At least two independent organizations are playing prominent roles in assessing the quality of charter schools. The Colorado League of Charter Schools, the Colorado state charter school association, is piloting a new self-assessment and accreditation tool for Colorado charter schools. For participating schools, the league will send out a peer-review team to develop "unique measures" of a school's success and create a three-to-five year review process. The intent is to serve a "critical friends" role for schools and also to provide good information to boards of education. The league's effort is in part to protect against perceived laxity by local school boards to require high standards, especially for the renewal of school charters.

Another such organization is the Illinois Facilities Fund (IFF), a nonprofit loan fund sponsored by the Chicago public school district. The IFF provides long-term loans to Chicago charter schools. In partnership with the Chicago school district's charter schools office, the IFF assesses the governance viability of charter school applicants and then provides assistance and continuing counseling to the schools.

Organizations that publicly support a charter school by lending money or partnering in other ways care about how the school is perceived by the community, whether that perception is shaped through newspaper articles or simply via word of mouth. These organizations have an interest, then, in at least appearing to give back to the community. They are often on the watch for cries of elitism, for instance, and so tend to go out of their way to make sure the schools they support serve diverse populations. Though some add money to charter school budgets, most make sure that total school funding does not exceed a level that could be matched by other public schools.

High-profile or controversial schools are more likely to be subjects of studies and visits by people who are looking for models for new schools or parents who are shopping for schools. These visitors add an extra element to accountability. Despite this constant stream of visitors, our researchers' requests for interviews were never turned down at schools with links to for-profit or nonprofit organizations.

Charter schools are often started by groups of parents who have little background in education or by teachers who have little business expertise. Unless these schools partner with nonprofit community groups or hire outside experts, they often face difficult barriers to success in creating effective schools. Schools we visited benefit greatly from expertise provided by their partner organizations. These organizations provide help by sending staff members to the school as guest lecturers, lending the school a business adviser, providing space for the school, and so on. Older nonprofit organizations often have experience building effective boards and creating lines of accountability within an organization. That experience, coupled with a promising educational approach, can create a very effective school.

Moreover, a for-profit management company's substantial financial backing may offer schools access to loans for school start-up and the ability to offer new or substantially renovated schools to students and parents, luxuries not available to most new groups. Though it is no guarantee of success, having access to these resources means a new school is more likely—and better able—to quickly focus on student learning.

Education Management Organizations

Education management organizations (EMOs), sometimes called management companies or service providers, are becoming increasingly common. EMOs range from those that provide specific, prescribed services such as payroll and financing (hereafter narrow providers) to those that are responsible for virtually every aspect of a charter school's operations (hereafter broad providers). Depending on the depth of their involvement, EMOs charge fees as small as a few percent of a school's operating budget to fees that encompass the school's entire budget. For the most part, narrow providers seem likely to increase a school's capacity to manage and account for funds, but they do not usually affect the school's organizational viability or educational effectiveness outside of their restricted domain.

Broad EMOs can have a more significant impact on a school's overall operations and academic responsibilities. Two examples can help to illustrate the benefits and potential risks of broad EMOs. We visited an Arizona school that is one of several schools run by the Leona Group, a large EMO operating primarily in Arizona and Michigan. The network of schools created by this EMO offers a unique benefit for information sharing and support. School leaders of all the Leona schools meet regularly and are able to gain assistance in their work from one another as well as Leona staff. Leona staff and school leaders also visit each school from time to time to offer feedback and evaluation.

Some decisions regarding the school are made within the school itself (for example, hiring and some curriculum decisions), while others are made at the Leona corporate office (including budgeting, hiring of the school leader, and other curriculum decisions). All the Leona schools in Arizona are based on a single charter, with one governing board consisting of two members based in Michigan and one who is a school leader in Arizona. From the perspective of Leona's authorizer, the Arizona Charter School Board, Leona is a well-respected organization seen as running solid schools. The school we visited had significant problems during its first year, when it was operating under a different name. By all accounts, the school was in complete disarray academically and organizationally. Leona staff replaced the principal when the school moved to a new location and began to expand. Since this change, the school has essentially been reinvented and has gone through some of the same struggles as other new charter schools, including last-minute hiring. Throughout these struggles, the Arizona Charter School Board has left it to Leona to intervene. Although the school files compliance and academic reports directly to the state, the charter school board monitors the school less closely than others because they trust Leona.

In Michigan, we visited a school that is operated by the National Heritage Academies (NHA). This group of elementary schools has a back-to-basics and moral education focus. In the 1998–1999 school year, NHA operated thirteen charter schools in Michigan. As with Leona, NHA school leaders meet regularly and discuss problems and policy issues facing their schools. Each NHA school has its own charter contract and its own governing board. While the governing board owns the charter contract, NHA owns each school's building and materials, and all staff members are employees of NHA, not the governing board. Hiring decisions are made by the school leader (who is selected by NHA), and many of the day-to-day decisions are made at the school level.

Broader issues such as the general curricular tools and the budget are made by NHA, which also sets policy for all its schools in a variety of areas. Not surprisingly, in this situation, some tension has arisen between the school's governing board and NHA over who makes what decisions.

These two examples illustrate several issues surrounding broad EMOs. The close connection between these two schools and their management organizations means that the school personnel (especially the school leaders) feel a strong sense of accountability to the larger organization. Both Leona and NHA have a much richer understanding of what is happening in a school than does the school's authorizing agency. The sense of accountability among the school leaders in each organization is particularly strong. They meet regularly, jointly work out issues regarding policies, and generally see their schools as closely connected with one another and with the parent organization. Leaders in individual schools feel that the successes or failures affect the reputations of the other schools and of the parent organization.

These relationships might have some negatives. First, schools may be less likely to develop a strong sense of internal accountability when they do not control such important issues as their budget and curriculum at the school site. At the Michigan school, there is clearly a strong sense of community, but there is also the frustration often found in traditional public schools for parents and others of being told that NHA, like a school district, will not allow certain changes. Second, authorizers who have a positive opinion of an EMO may be less likely to look critically at each school affiliated with that EMO during both the application and oversight processes. We have little evidence to prove or disprove either possibility; however, they are worth mentioning as areas for future study and caution. These two examples in no way capture the universe of broad EMOs, but they do reflect two approaches management organizations have taken and some of the questions that these approaches can raise for issues of accountability.

Using Political Connections to Buffer the School. The local and state politics associated with being a charter school can be intense. Local and state agency personnel may try to require compliance with laws from which the school should be exempt, a hostile school district may encourage fire marshals or building inspectors to give a new charter school a particularly difficult time with approval of its facility.

Outside organizations often have strong community ties that help a school stay focused on teaching and learning instead of spending time on appeasing a variety of external relations. A charter school with political connections through outside organizations is much better positioned to fight off spurious, politically motivated demands. In the traditional public school system, such political connections would likely be limited to schools in advantaged neighborhoods with high-powered parents. Charter schools' ability to work with outside organizations can lend that advantage to schools with less access to such power sources.

Increasing Access to Facilities. Charter schools most often must pay for their facilities costs out of the operating budgets. Facilities-related costs are often cited as the primary barrier to charter school start-up. The negative consequence is somewhat obvious: Rent costs money that schools then cannot spend on instruction. Rental costs keep some schools with promising educational ideas, but no access to appropriate facilities, from opening.

Partnerships with existing organizations often allow new schools, with no ability to float long-term bonds or to pay for up-front renovations, to gain access to partner-owned facilities. These partnerships also help educators to use their imagination about what facilities can be used as schools. The few states that are providing charter schools with capital moneys are seeing similarly positive results. In Arizona, the Goldwater Institute hosted a conference to bring together land developers and architects with charter school founders. Several innovative new partnerships have since developed, including a partnership between the Ball Foundation, which plans to open six new Arizona charter schools, and Continental Savings, which hopes to provide land for the Ball Foundation schools in new housing developments.

POTENTIAL DOWNSIDES OF VOLUNTARY ASSOCIATIONS. Despite the real advantage that chartering opens up to public school children by allowing and encouraging new schools to link with actors that operate outside the traditional public school establishment, this experiment—like others—comes with risks. In some circumstances, a heavy dependence on outside actors can confuse lines of accountability and decisionmaking, detract from the school's core mission, and attract unwanted attention.

Confusing Lines of Accountability and Decisionmaking. School governance is fragile. Its strength depends on the cohesiveness and focus of school leadership. When a school contracts with a management company, partners with a university, or takes a loan, each of these actions increases the sheer number of people who are providing input as to how the school ought to function.

More people involved in a school's operations also increases the potential for obscured responsibility and for disagreement. A school's approving agency, for instance, may be unclear whom to call if a problem arises. Parents may be unsure whom to contact if they have a complaint. A governing board may have trouble giving up control and may begin to interfere with a contractor's responsibilities or—equally problematic—may put too much trust in a contractor and not hold the organization responsible for its promises. The more complex the governance, the more difficult it becomes to establish clear lines of authority and accountability.

Contractors do not always use the same measures to judge school success as the governing board, teachers, parents, or the authorizing agency. Accreditation agents may or may not judge the school in ways that are consistent with the performance goals outlined in the school's charter. Financial lenders may be more concerned with financial stability than school improvement. Media attention as a result of a high-profile partner relationship may highlight controversy instead of communicate the strong points of a school.

Alliances with outside organizations can also complicate accountability. Some school governing boards hire professional management companies, including for-profit organizations such as Edison Schools and SABIS International, to run the school on a day-to-day basis. Such contracts are often necessary, particularly for governing boards that want to sponsor a school but do not think they have the expertise to create a good one on their own. Management companies also create clarity about school goals and methods, short-circuiting potentially long and laborious processes of school self-definition. But they add a powerful new player that affects all the internal relationships—among the governing board, school administrators, teachers, and parents—and often between the governing board and the government agency that issued the charter.

Management companies have their own interests (reputations to preserve, capacities to build, financial goals to meet) and ideas about what constitutes good teaching. Teachers hired by management companies must often meet well-established criteria and work on schedules dictated by the management company's philosophy, not determined within the school.

One education management company we interviewed appears to have struggled with how to define its relationship with its charter school boards. After several disputes over personnel matters and other issues the company saw as micromanagement from the board, the company is seeking what it terms "partnership" relationships as opposed to being seen as a contractor. To this end, the company purchased land for one of its schools as an indication of its investment. This partnership relationship, however, does not change the fact that the school's nonprofit governing board is legally responsible for the performance of the school.

In addition, some school governing boards and management companies have engaged in conflicts over who was in charge, especially when governing boards demanded to be able to pick and choose among instructional practices that management companies considered interdependent parts of a broader strategy. These conflicts, which in a small number of cases have led to firing of the management company, inevitably trickle down to the teaching staff and students. However, charter schools' need to maintain parent confidence tends to force the warring parties to reach some sort of resolution within a few months.

When a school subcontracts for services, especially for management of the educational program, it is critical that the contract itself be clear about who is responsible for what. Charter schools around the country are learning that lesson.

A new contracting guide published in 1999 by the Charter Friends National Network is designed to help charter school governing boards avoid these difficulties by developing clear contracts.[7] As it suggests, governing boards must not enter into relationships with outside organizations lightly. Charter school boards must understand their fiduciary duties and take them seriously.

Detracting from the School's Core Mission. If a charter school is overseen by a nonprofit board but has contracted with for-profit organizations, a potential always exists for conflict between the nonprofit's "mission" drive and the for-profit's "profit" drive. Even two nonprofit organizations might experience mission conflict. A small, parent-led school may partner, for instance, with an environmental community organization that can lend expertise and resources, but it then may feel pressure to spend more time on environmental excursions, for instance, than on reading.

In one case, a state charter school office called a social service nonprofit that had been providing jobs and general equivalency diploma (GED) preparation to suggest it apply for a charter. This organization had a longstanding relationship with the district because it educated harder-to-serve students and provided volunteer tutors to elementary schools for many years. The district was the authorizer and readily agreed to grant the charter. Though this organization has made the shift to managing a school relatively easily, it is experiencing difficulty learning how to run the elementary side of a K–12 school.

In both of these situations, strong school leadership must make sure that the school's instructional priorities to meet performance goals and other accountability requirements are fulfilled and that the school is able to stay focused on its core mission.

Attracting Unwanted Attention. The flip side of having strong political connections is often that a high-profile school attracts attention. While this can be an advantage, it can also create distractions for a school if not managed well. Schools with well-known partners are more likely to be written about in the newspapers and are more likely to attract researchers. Researchers and other visitors can quickly turn a serene school into a tourist attraction. The high-profile schools we visited have become skilled at scheduling visitors so that they do not interfere with the functioning of the school, but they remain aware of the mixed blessing of working with outside organizations.

The downsides are identifiable but manageable. Whether these relationships are positive or negative depends on whether the school has a clear sense of its mission and the leadership to use resources provided from the outside without losing its way, traits we believe all schools ought to have. On the whole, these relationships are less likely to fracture a school than are government categorical programs that come with many compliance and reporting strings attached.

These relationships, along with schools' new internal relationships between board and staff, represent important additions to public education. They potentially bring broader community financial and intellectual resources to bear on public education. They may encourage schools to be more responsive to parents and the general public. Most important, they make schools accountable to people and organizations that have a real stake in their success or failure.

Involuntary Relationships

In theory, charter school accountability to government is supposed to be confined to a school's relationship with its authorizer and to the content of its charter contract.[8] But in practice, this is almost never the case. In our review of state laws and regulations, our surveys, and our case studies, charter school accountability to government is clearly much more complex. We have found that

—Charter schools experience unexpected, and often unwelcome, intervention from governmental and political actors.

—Pressures from government intervenors and political interest groups can eclipse a charter school's relationships with parents, teachers, and even its authorizing agency.

Unexpected interventions are common. Other government agencies, besides the authorizing agency, also oversee charter schools, whether the authorizer wants them to or not. Almost half of the chartering agencies in our survey reported that they were aware of other agencies (local, state, or federal) that had conducted compliance reviews or audits of the schools they had chartered. However, this was far more likely among college- or university-based chartering agencies (86 percent) than among local districts (37 percent). This is probably because the primary outside agencies cited by the colleges and university chartering agencies were other university-related agencies. Only a few chartering agencies reported compliance reviews by either federal or state agencies.

Although these reviews and audits are sometimes politically motivated, many government agencies intervene in the operation of charter schools without any conscious intent to do harm. Many are simply working by the book, and because charter schools usually lack protectors within the bureaucracy, they are subject to harsher scrutiny than most public schools must endure.

Schools faced with mixed signals (and demands not contemplated in their charters) can be confused about whom they must listen to and what they must do. Charter schools that want to escape strict performance accountability can exploit such conflicting demands, hoping at reauthorization time to use a compliance defense. A school leader might say to an authorizer, for instance, "We did what we were told (which was different from what we had intended to do) and we are therefore not responsible for the results." Other schools have learned that if they have strong local constituencies and the expectations are unclear, their renewal is virtually assured.

However, charter schools that use this tactic risk their ability to put performance first. There is no way schools can meet all of these demands, so they must resort to focusing on those that satisfy immediate political needs. This compromise does not support a cohesive school organization.

In the course of this study we talked with a mayor's aide whose job it was to coordinate the work of city agencies so that public schools undergoing renovations could open on time. The aide convened meetings of small-city inspectors—health, fire, buildings, and so on—some months in advance of a school's reopening to stress the mayor's interest in making sure all inspections were done and signed off on time. As the aide explained, without the mayor's initiative, something was bound to go wrong—inspections done late, rules interpreted too literally, lenient options overlooked. With the mayor's expression of interest, city inspectors could be counted on to use their discretion in ways consistent with the school's opening.

In the absence of such powerful good offices, charter schools can be disrupted in ways that regular public schools seldom experience, whether or not the public agencies involved bear them any ill will.

Interventions can compromise accountability to authorizers, parents, teachers, and donors. In many cases, schools and authorizing agencies are subject to demands from state and federal agencies, teachers unions, and other interest groups fearing that charter school practices might set precedents that weaken their positions elsewhere.

Charter schools in Michigan, for example, have faced a very complex web of government accountability. Teachers unions and other organizations critical of charter schools have called in government agencies as diverse as the fire marshal, the fair employment practices commission, and the state auditor to inspect schools. At the request of members elected to the state board of education and the state legislature, the state auditor conducted an unprecedented review of Central Michigan University (CMU), the state agency that has authorized the majority of charter schools. In the first few years after the law passed under a Republican administration, teachers unions also pressured school districts to refuse to hire any teachers from CMU's school of education until a provision was added to the state law forbidding them to do this.

The results of this highly charged environment are twofold: It creates confusion over who is responsible for oversight, and it creates transaction costs that can cripple schools. While charter school sponsors are supposedly responsible only for monitoring the terms of charter school contracts, the contracts reference the entire state law and regulatory code. Multiple government agencies also have responsibility to investigate complaints, and thus they are also involved in monitoring. The result, according to many schools we interviewed, is a high level of duplication of oversight.

The two-person charter school office in Massachusetts is often the focal point of competing political forces. Sole authorization and revocation powers rest with the Massachusetts Board of Education (MBOE). This nine-person board was appointed by Republican governor William F. Weld and his successor, Paul Cellucci. The MBOE sets policy for the Massachusetts Department of Education and more specifically the charter school office, a unit within the department. Charter schools are the trophy of the Weld and Cellucci administrations' education initiatives.

A countermove by Democrats has been to tighten oversight of all charter school operations. In 1997 the Democratically controlled legislature created oversight commissions to examine (1) the charter school office for ethics violations, (2) how the average cost per student was being allocated, (3) whether the charter schools were innovative, (4) what was happening in the schools (site visits on top of the site visits the charter school office was already conducting), and (5) fiscal audits of individual schools and the charter school office itself. After two years of looking, state auditor Joe DeNucci, a Democrat, reported that the South Shore Charter School had bad book-keeping practices in its first two years of operation. The report does not provide evidence that the funds were misspent and also indicates that the problem was corrected in the school's third and fourth years, but it still made the front page of the Metro section of the *Boston Globe*.

Nationwide, another political battle is being waged over how charter schools should interpret special education laws. In Chicago and Massachusetts, organizations concerned about the rights of special needs students have intervened in charter schools, charging that the authorizing agencies (and the children's parents) had agreed to instructional programs not following federal guidelines or that charter school buildings were not up to strict accessibility codes.

Schools and authorizing agencies ignore political wrangling and interventions from diverse government agencies at their peril. Some can tie up a school or an authorizing agency in compliance reviews or litigation. Heavy new transaction costs can kill a struggling charter school.

Other government agencies, especially state education departments, are understandably confused about how they should deal with charter schools. Though some have the impression that they are to keep hands off, others assume that charter schools, like all other public schools, must fill out standard financial, attendance, and service reports and account in detail for the use of funds. Administrators of federal categorical programs assume that charter schools must use funds and deliver services much the way other schools do. Some local and state administrators may be deliberately testing charter school operators to see how much of the normal regulatory burden they will accept. But most simply reason that if other public schools must submit a particular report or plan, a charter school must be similarly obligated.

Conclusion

In an environment that allows almost anyone to intervene in the life of a charter school at almost any time, charter schools must rely on those who are in positions of power to take a leadership role in defining their responsibilities and buffering them from diverse interest group and agency demands.

Central Michigan University has eliminated some of the ambiguity about oversight by being proactive about helping charter schools navigate the regulatory environment. CMU concluded that the state's requirements were often unclear and that because separate state bureaus administer different rules, no one can readily describe all the regulations schools must obey or all the reports they must file. CMU therefore took responsibility for identifying all rules and all required reports and informing CMU-sponsored schools what had to be done and when. In future years, charter schools will receive CD-ROMs with complete reporting schedules and all necessary forms, filled out with the previous year's data and ready for easy amendment and electronic filing. By this method, CMU has made compliance obligations clearer and less intrusive.

In the early years of implementation of Massachusetts's charter school law, then governor Weld oversaw charter schools directly through his own Office of Education. His secretary of education actively ran interference for newly founded charter schools that were being blocked from starting because of local permitting problems. Weld's successor continued to support and protect the integrity of the Massachusetts charter school initiative.

This reliance on key political and bureaucratic champions for charter schools is a reality. Whether it helps or hinders a solid accountability system is a different question. When high-level politicians and community leaders have their names associated with a particular reform, it can provide a positive incentive to make sure the reform does not simply wash away. However, high-level politicians may be resistant to critical analysis of performance that is healthy for any new program. In Arizona, for instance, the state agency has come under fire for not providing sufficient monitoring for parents to get good information about the market of charter schools.

Definite resolution of these issues will require clearer laws and clearer implementation. Some of this is already occurring. Legislators who are drafting newer charter school laws are learning from the experiences of states that enacted ambiguous statutes. Implementers around the country are sharing lessons about what has worked and what has not. For the time being, charter schools and authorizing agencies will have to feel their way, alert to the costs of conceding anyone's right to make demands, whether contemplated in their charters or not.

CHAPTER SIX

Recommendations

Charter school laws put schools in a situation of mixed accountability; they must answer to private parties as well as to government in pursuit of a public purpose. The public purpose is student learning. In theory, charter schools' accountabilities serve that public purpose—parents, teachers, and other private parties, as well as authorizers, care about student learning and reward or punish schools accordingly. Also in theory, schools are more likely to attain that public purpose if they are accountable to all those parties than if they are accountable to only one of them. No party, not even government, knows exactly what students need to know, nor can any party, not even government, be completely trusted to act purely in students' interest.

Using mixed accountability mechanisms to serve public ends is not a new idea. Public utilities, for example, are accountable both to government and to their investors. In recent years they have also become accountable to customers, who are free to switch from one provider to another. Publicly funded social services are now delivered both by government agencies and by private organizations. These groups are accountable to government via contracts but also remain accountable to their boards and to parents. Even conventional public school systems make promises to get private donations and rely on volunteer effort by parents and teachers. These are all examples of enterprises that combine government oversight and private accountability in pursuit of broader public ends.[1]

By design, charter schools must reconcile pressures from many sources. They depend on many different parties—authorizing agencies, families, teachers, donors, volunteer governing boards, and other government agencies—each of whom has reason to expect evidence of performance. Each external party hopes the school will produce high levels of student performance, but some have their own peculiar concerns. Authorizers are also concerned about financial propriety, teachers about job security and working conditions, families about safety and caring, other government agencies about maintaining regimes of regulation that they think benefit their particular clients, and so on.

Despite many false starts and some outright failures, charter schools are learning to face the problems of multidirectional accountability. They are helped by the fact that the most significant parties to whom they are accountable—parents and teachers—care more about maintaining a school climate conducive to learning than any other dimension of school performance. Though some authorizers, other government agencies, and assistance groups create pressures that do not reinforce the schools' focus on teaching and learning, on the whole the schools we studied are creating internal accountability mechanisms that allow them to deliver enough of what everyone cares about to maintain their charters and survive financially. Though some charter schools cannot handle all the pressures on them and thus close, charter laws allow other schools to form and, potentially, learn from others' failures.

Nevertheless, there are still unresolved issues about charter school accountability.

—Some charter schools have managed to produce acceptable student outcomes but are still a long way from creating strong internal accountability arrangements and stable working relationships between the governing boards and management.

—Only a few of the hundreds of legally designated charter authorizing agencies have faced their own responsibilities in holding charter schools accountable. Some authorizers fall back on process and compliance monitoring and avoid acting on measures of student performance, instead of opening themselves up to the criticism that they will not close or replace any of the conventional public schools for which they are also responsible.

—Charter schools can be exposed to forms of pressure and coercion from other government agencies that other public schools do not encounter. These agencies often hold individual charter schools to standards of racial balance, service to handicapped children, and facilities quality that normally apply to whole school districts, not to individual public schools.

No one could expect all these problems to be solved within five years of the beginning of such a radical shift in methods of public service provision. Moreover, charter schools, their supporters, and some authorizers (including the states of Colorado and Massachusetts, special-purpose authorizing agencies in the District of Columbia and Michigan, and school districts in Chicago and Colorado) are making headway.

In general, charter schools' multidirectional accountability can work, in the all-important sense of promoting effective instruction for children. For this to happen, however, charter schools must be more than neutral registers of the external pressures upon them. They must be bona fide organizations, capable of galvanizing the effort of adults and children in pursuit of a mission and using data and expertise to solve problems. In short, if a school is to be externally accountable, it must also be internally accountable.

Charter schools develop internal accountability because they need to do so. Internal accountability is necessary because

—A school receives public funds only if it meets the conditions of its charter; that is, to deliver a coherent instructional program, show a government authorizer that students are learning, and maintain equitable admissions practices.

—A school must compete for students, whose families send them only if the school provides credible instruction and maintains a motivating, safe, and caring climate.

—A school must compete for teachers, who can choose schools that they believe are stable enough to pay them and that provide a satisfying professional climate.

Internal accountability is possible because

—Schools control funds and can therefore decide how to allocate resources between instruction and other objectives. They can also purchase the kinds of materials and advice they need to improve instruction.

—Schools have hiring authority over staff, which allows them to select the combination of skills the staff needs to manage its instructional program and gives schools the leverage they need to ensure that all faculty members work to provide the kind of instruction promised.

—Schools control their schedules and staff work assignments, and they can adapt programs to the needs of students and respond to information about their own performance.

However, our research shows that these conditions are not in themselves sufficient to create internal accountability. Some charter schools encounter all these conditions and still fail to become internally accountable. Becoming internally accountable requires something more: compelling ideas about what makes a good school; leadership to help staff, parents, and the governing board converge on a common image of the school; and continued hard work to update general agreement about the school's purposes and methods and apply it to current circumstances.

People outside the school can create the conditions that force a school to be internally accountable and enable a school to take responsibility for its results. Outsiders can even help the school community converge on shared ideas about good instruction. The fact that a charter school must establish enough guiding principles up front to write a compelling proposal starts it on the way toward establishing internal accountability. But many charter schools nonetheless struggle, and a few ultimately fail, to develop this mechanism. Based on our research we do not have a complete theory of how schools develop internal accountability. We can, however, identify the ways that key actors, both within and outside the school, enable and help schools develop internal accountability.

How Key Actors Can Improve Charter School Accountability

Most actors care more about whether a school gives children a positive learning environment and provides effective instruction than about whether it is punctilious about following rules. However, rules are part of life. The key to the success of charter schools—and to public education in general—is to find a way to reconcile the compliance pressure on schools with their need to focus on issues of teaching and learning. To make this possible, all parties must accept some responsibilities.

Charter School Governing Boards

Charter school governing boards need to understand that boards of directors must follow David Osborne and Ted Gaebler's dictum to "steer, not row" in formulating the school's mission and making decisions that set long-term directions, such as hiring the school head and establishing the criteria against which his or her performance will be judged.[2] Directors who are also school founders must accept the fact that, like parents, they must learn to let go. Stable and productive board-management relationships depend on the board's acceptance of the limitations of its steering role, supporting management whenever possible and replacing, not hobbling, managers who are not effective.

New boards must expect a serious shakedown period that requires continual clarification of mission, governance relationships, and staffing. Neither boards nor staffs can always operate on the basis of consensus, and some conflicts might be serious enough to lead some board members or school managers to depart. In several charter schools we visited, as with many good private schools, the departure of board members who cannot accept the way a school is evolving is an important step toward a coherent school. The board must continually ask whether its actions are strengthening or weakening the instructional program and whether its actions clarify or blur the divisions of responsibility on which internal accountability is built.

Charter School Leaders

Charter school leaders need to seize the initiative on external accountability. Though some charter school leaders think the less they have to do with their authorizers the better, avoidance leads to trouble. School leaders need to initiate contact with their authorizers, define the terms under which they hope authorizers will hold them accountable, and create a flow of relevant information. Several schools we visited did this by starting conversations about renewal requirements long before their authorizer had given the question any thought. Some charter school leaders insisted on attending all districtwide academic meetings for principals whether they were required to be there or not. These school leaders saw those meetings as an opportunity to show their districts that they were interested in learning from others and in sharing their mistakes and successes with others.

Schools that avoid assessment or resist tests that the government is clearly authorized to require only increase the likelihood that government will do what comes naturally—try to control the situation by imposing new rules, demanding compliance, and imposing penalties. Schools in states that require standards-based testing can critique the tests, but they must not resist administering them. School leaders must avoid first encouraging staff opposition to the tests and later telling staff they have no choice but to go along.

School leaders must also take the initiative in creating well-informed expectations among parents, teachers, and governing board members. Leaders must clearly communicate to parents and teachers what the school intends to accomplish and what it will not attempt. Vaguely characterizing the school as a happy place that values diversity and helps everyone learn does not discourage parents and teachers from maintaining irreconcilable fantasies about what the school will be. The school must be characterized clearly enough so that people can know what it will not do, and so that people whose expectations cannot be met will look elsewhere. No school can meet every need and provide every service or activity. The board of a Massachusetts charter school said, "Some parents were shocked that we didn't have a band, even though we never mentioned having one. We had to tell these parents that we had put our money elsewhere, and if band was essential for them, they could get it at another school."

Attaining this degree of clarity takes time. No one can know in advance all the expectations that people might carry with them into the school. But at every juncture, school leaders serve everyone best by creating clarity, not ambiguity.

Educators accustomed to conventional public schools, in which staff and parents are assigned to a school and must find ways to live with their differences, have learned to paper over conflicts with glittering generalities. Charter school leaders must operate differently, constructing specific expectations, selecting and socializing staff, and creating internal divisions of responsibility that allow the school to meet them. This requires setting action priorities on the basis of hard performance data, not staff politics. It also implies, as many charter schools have learned, that some staff departures, however painful, can increase school unity.

Parents

Parents need to know what to expect from a school and effectively demand what was promised. Charter schools need to be held to their promises, and parents who insist that they do so strengthen their school. But parents who import their own secret hopes, especially for instructional programs, facilities, and extracurricular activities that a charter school lacks the capacity to deliver, only diffuse the efforts of board and staff. No matter how good the reputation of a charter school, parents should take time to get a real grip on the school's mission, instructional approach, and focus before enrolling his or her child. If the school is already up and running, parents should spend a day visiting classrooms, interviewing teachers and other parents, and talking with the principal and board members.

Parents need to become wise consumers. Parents need to understand that not every charter school is for every child. It is their responsibility to perform due diligence before enrolling a child in a school. Parents need to ask questions: What will students experience every day? What will the school's climate and academic standards be? What kind of help will children get when they are struggling? What is expected of families? Charter schools themselves can help parents make sure they thoroughly understand the school's program by hosting an orientation for prospective parents that simulates a virtual day in the life of a student at that school. One school we visited in Michigan found this a successful way to orient parents in real terms.

Teachers

Teachers need to understand that joining a charter school is an opportunity to change the type of educational relationship teachers have with students and other teachers. Charter schools are problem-solving organizations, and the survival of the school depends on each teacher's success. Teachers and leaders must consider themselves as co-owners and co-managers, not as bureaucrats with limited responsibility. Teachers in new charter schools work long hours, but as one told us, "This work is not for everybody, but this is what it takes to build the kind of school where I want to work."

Like parents, teachers need to perform due diligence about whether a charter school's expectations match theirs. They also need to hold board members and school leaders to their promises about instructional quality, school climate, and professional development opportunities. Teachers strengthen schools if they demand quality. But teachers must expect to be challenged and to work under performance pressure. Those responsible for hiring at charter schools can help teachers understand the demands required at those schools by advertising the job effectively and being clear to prospective hires about the nature of the job. One school we visited is explicit in its desire for teachers who are adaptable and who like constant change. Being comfortable with change may not be a prerequisite for all charter schools, but teachers and those who hire them should know what kind of teacher is most likely to succeed at a particular school.

Authorizers

Authorizers need to take their responsibilities toward charters seriously. School districts, in particular, need to overcome habits of letting schools slide until something dire happens. This requires creating routines for monitoring and assessing schools and rules of thumb to use early in a school's development to distinguish schools that are having normal start-up problems from those that are seriously at risk of failing to deliver. Authorizers should consider creating or contracting for inspectorates to provide ongoing assessments of schools, as has the Massachusetts charter schools office.

Authorizers must fulfill their public duties to ensure that charter schools are held accountable for performance and to protect students from failing schools. This requires ways of measuring whether children are learning. It does not require exhaustive measurement of every aspect of a school's operation, but it does require sharp, valid, and tamper-proof measures of student learning outcomes, especially in core subjects. Parents and teachers can be trusted to assess and react to important but hard-to-measure school attributes such as climate and morale. But authorizers must collect and act on hard measures of whether students are learning.

Authorizers must also adapt to the realities of dealing with schools that are independent organizations responsible for demonstrating student performance. Schools cannot be expected to develop as educational institutions if they are constantly surprised by rules and constraints newly discovered by disorganized authorizers. Charter schools can live with rules, but rules must be stable and the accompanying administrative burdens predictable. Unstable rules and sporadic enforcement can drive schools in one of two directions: toward either slavish compliance to the rule of the day or arrogant disregard of compliance obligations. The former sacrifices school effectiveness, while the latter can promote school effectiveness but can lead to inequities and misuses of funds that discredit not only charter schooling, but also public education in general. Authorizers that handle this tension well provide a list of all required rules and regulations in the initial charter and offer a written explanation of the process by which the agency intends to enforce those rules. Acknowledging that Michigan's charter school law did not exempt charter schools from state reporting requirements, Central Michigan University accepted responsibility for making these requirements clear. It found that no one in the Michigan Department of Education could say what all the requirements were, so CMU did its own analysis and provided its charter schools with user-friendly electronic filing forms.

State Governments

State governments need to hold authorizers accountable for their responsibilities. All states that allow local school districts to charter schools must understand that districts are not accustomed to holding schools accountable for performance. Many need help understanding their responsibilities, and they need exposure to districts that have learned how to fulfill these responsibilities. State-funded professional development for administrators responsible for charter school oversight and for school board members is essential, but no state has accepted this responsibility.

States need to provide enough guidance and training so that a conscientious authorizer can determine whether it is fulfilling its responsibilities toward potential and current charter operators. States also need to make sure local districts and other authorizers face negative consequences if they do not follow the intent of state law in processing charter school applications and overseeing charter school performance.

Federal Government

The federal government needs to put its own house in order about charter schools. Though the federal government is subsidizing charter school start-ups and encouraging enactment of state charter school laws, it is also letting federal agencies deal with charter schools in needlessly disruptive ways. Though there is nothing about state charter school laws that should exempt charter schools from civil rights laws, government agencies need to adapt to the differences between independent public schools held accountable for performance and dependent public schools operated by public bureaucracies.

For some purposes, the federal government has dealt with charter schools as if they were school districts. This has meant that individual charter schools have been required to offer special education programs that school districts, not individual schools, normally provide. These requirements can be financially lethal to charter schools, which receive fixed per-pupil payments and do not have large central offices that can spread the costs of serving a few extraordinarily expensive students among scores of schools. In conventional public education, no one school must provide services appropriate to every disabled child. It is enough for the school district to provide appropriate services at some place in the district that is accessible to the student. Charter schools need to be able to make similar arrangements, either by relying on school districts to provide special education or by forming consortia in which different charter schools provide different special education services.

Similarly, the federal government needs to adapt, but not abandon, its requirements for racial balance in schools. Federal agencies have blocked the opening of some charter schools that do not reflect the racial balance in the larger communities they serve, even though nearby conventional public schools were even less racially balanced. Charter schools' racial balances should fit within the range of school-by-school variation observable in neighboring school districts. They should not, however, face more demanding federal requirements than individual schools in districts that courts and federal enforcers do not officially consider illegally segregated.

These issues will not be settled by individual federal agencies acting on their own initiative. The impetus to rationalize federal policy toward charter schools must come from a higher place—from the secretary of education or the White House domestic adviser.

Friends of the Charter School Movement

Friends of the charter school movement need to help government agencies and private actors support and effectively evaluate charter schools. Foundations, charter school associations, and resource centers should direct investments to help charter schools develop strong governing boards and internal accountability mechanisms such as self-assessment models, effective grievance policies, and staff evaluations. State and national associations should help disseminate best practices on internal accountability to other charter schools and to other public schools.

Those who hope to see the charter school movement expand and thrive must also work to expose charter schools to technical tools that help them get the kinds of data they need to be held accountable.[3] Likewise, friends must help charter school authorizers and evaluators develop new capacities to measure school progress, instead of relying on traditional government compliance evaluations.

Perhaps most important, charter friends need to develop effective ways to help parents and government evaluate the progress of their children and their children's schools. Efforts in these areas are emerging and should be fostered. In Rochester, New York, a local foundation has provided planning grants to schools on the condition that they adopt a common assessment model that can be used to create a charter school report card. The Charter School Development Center at California State University offers accountability training and materials for authorizers as well as schools. The Walton Foundation is funding a multistate project to develop and disseminate new accountability methods for charter schools.

While statewide associations and resource centers can do much to support strong accountability and strong schools, these organizations have their limitations. Their main mission is to help individual schools get started and thrive. A new statewide independent nongovernment entity must also serve a more specific role. Such an organization would be charged simply with defending the integrity of the state's charter school law. It would act as a watchdog for a state's faithful implementation of the charter law, fight unnecessary new regulatory demands, help central office and authorizing agency staff to shift from a control mode to a support mode, and help develop multiple sources of information about charter schools (that is, media, associations, parent groups, and so on).

Implications

Our analysis of charter school accountability is a snapshot in time. The charter school movement is growing and developing too quickly for any analysis to be an accurate representation of the landscape for long. Providers, consumers, and regulators of charter schools are becoming more sophisticated in their new roles but are also struggling with important challenges—some anticipated, some not. The relevance of our study therefore goes far beyond the question of whether charter schools are accountable in the ways envisioned by early advocates.

CHAPTER SEVEN

Learning from Charter School Accountability

Charter schools are one attempt to answer the question that dominates current debates about K–12 education policy: How can public agencies ensure that schools are educating children effectively without imposing burdens that weaken schools' effectiveness? In general, we have shown that charter schools' multidirectional accountability can work, in the all-important sense of promoting effective instruction for children.

A much larger national initiative—standards-based reform—also addresses the problem of making schools public yet effective. Supporters of standards-based reform often regard charter schools advocates as rivals, and vice versa. Bruce Fuller, for example, casts the difference between charters and standards sharply, as between totally decentralized (charters) and strongly centralized (standards) approaches to public oversight. However, a few education policy analysts consider themselves supporters of both standards and charters. (Chester E. Finn and Diane Ravitch are among those who strongly favor both.)

Fuller's characterization notwithstanding, standards-based reform is not purely a movement toward centralization. It does have an element of centralization (statewide standards for student learning in core subjects), but it also has an element of decentralization (increased school freedom to use time and resources in any way necessary to promote student learning). Chartering is also not a purely decentralizing reform. It relies heavily on public authorities to act decisively to cancel the charters of failed schools and to charter new schools that will serve groups of students whose needs are unmet.

The supporters of charter schools and standards-based reform differ on matters of taste. Charter supporters are comfortable with entrepreneurship by groups of teachers, parents, and administrators, and with parent choice. Standards-based reform supporters are nervous about relying on entrepreneurship and family choice, though most are comfortable if these phenomena are limited to a fixed group of district-operated schools. Standards-based reform supporters are comfortable with maintaining the existing structure of school boards, central offices, and central hiring of teachers, though many believe that central office spending should be reduced so that school control of funds can increase and that schools should choose teachers on the basis of fit, not seniority.

These differences in taste have fewer practical consequences than most people think. Charter schools and standards-based education are different faces of the same reform. Both seek schools capable of problem solving, free to allocate time and money in response to students' needs. Both need authorizers capable of competent, consistent, performance-based oversight. Both require that authorizers have some fair and explicit mechanism by which to judge school performance. Both require authorities to oversee schools individually, because schools face different challenges and have different track records of performance.

The failure of public agencies to develop capacities for school oversight is as much a problem for standards-based reform as for charter schools. Both require states and school districts to stop layering on process requirements and evaluating schools on the basis of rule compliance and scandal avoidance. Neither can survive if authorities play favorites and demand less stringent performance of schools that they control directly than of schools that operate with greater independence.[1] Government's success or failure in learning to play this role will determine, as Richard F. Elmore has written of standards-based reform, whether "we . . . get the version of standards-based reform that advocates envision, or we . . . get a corrupted and poorly thought-out evil twin."[2]

Why Chartering Needs Standards

Chartering is not a pure market system that lets schools live or die on whether they can attract students. Though chartering provides parental choice, it also assumes performance-based public oversight. Chartering requires public authorities that can judge whether students are learning and schools are fulfilling their charters. These authorities must be able to cancel a charter that is not benefiting children and to charter new schools to serve children whose schools have failed them.

Standards provide a common metric against which individual charter schools can be judged. They also enable public agencies to oversee diverse portfolios of schools. Schools can differ in many ways as long as they demonstrate that students are making progress toward attainment of standards. State standards need not be the only basis on which schools are judged. Many charter schools want to be judged on such measures as student retention and graduation rates, proportion of students making normal progress toward graduation, proportion of students failing multiple courses, and graduates' performance at the next higher level of education. But standards provide the common basis on which diverse schools can all be judged alike.

Conflict within the charter school movement has masked its dependency on standards. Some enthusiasts see charter schooling as a way to get away from the trappings of regular public education, including the use of conventional student achievement tests and other performance measures. These teachers and parents—most of whom favor approaches to education in which students construct knowledge through exploration instead of learning according to a fixed schedule—dislike any form of comparative performance measurement. They feel that it takes time away from learning, narrows the focus of instruction, and provides discouraging and inappropriately negative feedback to disadvantaged students.

Hoping to avoid achievement testing, some charter school leaders prefer to rely on their ability to win a future political struggle. Some are even willing to accept new mandates not contemplated by their charters as a way of building up political credits.

Such efforts to avoid testing put charter schools at great risk. When charter school leaders reject all testing, they give new life to the compliance mentality, under which a school's existence depends on avoiding conflict with persons of influence and maintaining a spotless record of rule following.

Except under a pure voucher system, in which parental satisfaction would be the only basis for accountability, there must be some basis of public oversight. Both charters and standards-based reform assume that school performance is measurable and can be fairly assessed and compared. They absolutely require some efficient measures of school performance. These need not all be based on student test performance. Skills demonstrations, written products, and more authentic measures of student outcomes such as performance at higher levels of education are highly desirable. Moreover, charter school operators have every right to object to tests that are biased or are poorly aligned with state standards. But it is in their interest, just as it is in the interest of supporters of standards-based reform, to suggest what common, objective measures of student performance should be used instead.

Both chartering and standards-based reform recognize the public interest in schooling, in ensuring that students learn basic skills, prepare for responsible lives as earners and citizens, and understand basic democratic values. Both require government agencies—normally local school boards—to monitor individual school performance, promote school improvement, adapt school offerings to meet emerging needs, and protect children in schools that do not work.[3]

With respect to accountability, no conflict exists between standards and chartering; in fact, the two reinforce each other. Standards provide a basic structure for valuing school outcomes and for characterizing the performance of individual schools. Chartering creates a process whereby districts can act on information about school performance, making it clear that performance (as judged according to standards) is the basis on which the district rewards, targets intervention in, and, on occasion, replaces schools. Chartering also enables districts to work directly on the supply of schools in their locality, creating new ones to meet emerging needs (for example, as demographics and technology change) and setting up new schools in areas that are poorly served by existing public schools.

What Chartering Can Add to Standards-Based Reform

While charter school advocates have given a great deal of thought to the problems of individual school accountability, leaders of the standards-based reform movement have given it relatively little. This is understandable because standards-based reformers started at the top of the system and have only recently gotten beyond the problems of standards setting and test development. A few states—Kentucky, Massachusetts, North Carolina, Texas, and Washington—have begun to consider what it means to hold individual schools accountable for what their children learn. However, as states take on the problem of standards-based school accountability, they will need to draw some lessons from the charter schools' experience. These lessons are of two kinds: lessons about the environment of rules, funding, and assistance that make it possible for individual schools to take responsibility for student performance; and lessons about the importance of schools' being accountable to many different entities.

Lessons about the Environment of Rules, Funding, and Assistance

Chartering creates three circumstances that promote school accountability. First, it creates performance incentives by making it clear that all the adults in a school have stakes in the school's success (or failure) in educating students. Second, it creates school freedom of action, allowing school staff to use their time and money in the ways they believe are likely to have the greatest effect on student learning. Third, it creates opportunities for both private and public investments in school capacity, including teaching methods, materials, and staff training and recruitment.

Schools cannot be accountable under standards-based reform unless these circumstances exist.[4] Even when states are clear about what they expect students to learn, schools are not accountable if teachers and administrators stand to gain or lose nothing no matter how well or badly their students perform. In the absence of performance incentives, standards-based reform is purely exhortation. Moreover, when states set standards and are determined to reward and penalize individual schools based on what they add to student learning, schools are unlikely to improve unless teachers and administrators are free to change their instructional programs to make the best possible uses of students' and teachers' time and talent. In the absence of freedom of action, standards-based reform establishes a double bind: Schools must improve, but they must not change.

Finally, even when states set standards, create incentives, and offer freedom of action, schools are unlikely to improve unless teachers and administrators learn about more effective ways of providing instruction, have the information necessary to make good choices, and can purchase the assistance and materials (including technology) necessary to give students the full benefit of improved methods. In the absence of investment, schools with low capacity experience pressure to improve, are free to change, but are limited by the skills and knowledge of the adults who work there.

Chartering provides performance incentives, freedom of action, and investments and capacities to extreme degrees. Schools in which children do not learn can lose their charters and be forced to close. Schools are supposed to be bound only by the terms of their charters. They also receive real dollars on a per-pupil basis and are free to allocate them among staff, rent, materials, and other expenses. Charter schools can invest their funds in teacher training and other instructional improvement strategies. They can also solicit funds and other help from private parties.

Does standards-based reform require states to go that far? What if schools were just praised or criticized for performance? What if all the current rules and contracts stayed intact and schools were simply invited to ask for the waivers they want? What if schools did not control money and hiring decisions but could ask for waivers? What if schools did not control money but a wise and benevolent central office administration made investments for them?

These are understandable questions because the changes implied by performance accountability, school freedom of action, and investments in school capacity are wrenching. They imply that school boards, central offices, and teachers unions must do their jobs differently. However, modest measures are almost certainly not sufficient. Under earlier efforts to decentralize public schools, districts (under the banner site-based management) typically had little effect on student learning because they did not go far enough. Though some schools seized the opportunities provided by district site-based management initiatives, the majority changed very little, if at all, in part because there was no strong pressure for them to change.

As Anthony S. Bryk and others reported after a study of six cities' decentralization efforts, few schools change just because they have the freedom to do so.[5] In the absence of performance incentives, those teachers and administrators who want to change their schools are hamstrung by others who feel no need to change.

New York City's Community District #2, led by Anthony Alvarado, is sometimes offered as an example of a standards-based reform based solely

LEARNING FROM CHARTER SCHOOL ACCOUNTABILITY 103

on investments in teacher training. Major increases in the amounts of money spent on professional development for literacy instruction were keys to that district's success. However, those investments were combined with a massive turnover of teachers and principals who did not want to cooperate with the district's initiative. Such staff changes were possible in a community district that could easily export teachers and principals to jobs in the rest of New York City's million-student public school system. Moreover, other factors were at work in District #2. The superintendent created clear agreements between the district and individual schools, which focused on improvement strategy and scope of site-level discretion. Within these de facto charters, school site leaders had significant freedom of action. Though District #2 is not a charter district, it exemplifies a reform holding schools accountable for performance and employing a combination of incentives, school freedom of action, and investments in school capacity.

Lessons about Effective Oversight

Even under the best-designed standards-based reforms, few school districts and state education agencies are structured to oversee a system of performance-based accountability. They lack data and analytic capacity for individualized judgment of schools, relying instead on one-size-fits-all requirements for accountability. In many cases, this has led to a backlash against standards and accountability systems.[6] Lacking strong analytic tools to assess school performance, states and districts shy away from acting decisively toward failed schools. And fundamentally, the relationship between school and district is bound by traditions of a top-down or one-way accountability relationship that is extremely difficult to overcome. Central office staff and governing officials are not used to letting schools make their own decisions and mistakes, and schools and parents are not used to taking responsibility for their own decisions and mistakes.

For school boards to oversee schools on the basis of student performance, as standards-based reform requires, they must imitate special-purpose chartering agencies in

—Learning to negotiate performance agreements with individual schools that take account of a school's unique focus and goals without sacrificing bottom-line objective measures. The accountability agreements developed by Chicago and Massachusetts are strong models. The vague school improvement plans now required by districts could be replaced by such concrete accountability plans.

—Training oversight boards and central office staff to monitor data and set policy direction instead of creating directives. The Charter School Development Center in Sacramento, California, is a model here.

—Learning how to make refined judgments of school progress via inspectorates and self-assessment processes instead of letting politics alone guide decisionmaking. The new National Association of Charter School Authorizers is building a network of such knowledge. As well, excellent new guidebooks for charter authorizing agencies are available.[7]

—Drawing from the experience of chartering agencies about how to assess proposals for new schools.[8] This knowledge could enable standards-based districts and states to become smart buyers when it comes time to reconstitute or provide alternatives to a failed school.

Lessons about Balanced Accountability

Charter schools are accountable in several directions, not just one. They are accountable to their authorizing agencies, but they must also retain the confidence of parents, teachers, and private donors. School leaders know that losing their charter is a sentence of death, and so they carefully manage relationships with their authorizing agencies. Being accountable in several directions strengthens, not weakens, charter schools as educational institutions. School leaders lack the time and resources to pander separately to each of their constituencies. The only way they can manage their accountability relationships is to make sure that students have the learning experiences promised and that the instructional program is effective. Thus the need to balance accountability forces school leaders to attend to their most important obligation to authorizers and parents. It also requires schools to create a climate in which teachers can work effectively. Charter schools that do not balance their accountabilities by focusing on quality instruction are always in danger of losing their charters, or parental or teacher support.

The original theory of standards-based reform does not include this concept of multidirectional accountability. It assumes that other parties—families, teachers, and potential donors—work through the oversight agency. The agency, for example, a local school board, is supposed to balance the interests of different parties and act accordingly.

However, as states try to design standards-based school accountability systems, the original theory does not stand up well. Schools that cannot have direct relationships of mutual choice with families and teachers are constrained in ways that limit their effectiveness. Schools that cannot reap the benefits of private investments cannot innovate as much as those that can accept ideas and resources from any source that has something to offer.

A revised theory of accountability under standards-based reform, exemplified by Sarah Brooks's paper on the strong schools theory of accountability, comes close to chartering in arguing that schools should have direct accountability relationships with parties other than their government oversight agencies.[9] Family choice of schools, reciprocal choice between teachers and schools, and school freedom to enter investment and assistance agreements with independent parties can all enhance schools' performance accountability.

FAMILY CHOICE. Though family choice creates pressures for schools, it also increases their freedom of action. If no family is compelled to send its children to a particular school, no school needs to meet absolutely every family expectation. Schools can (and must) be clear about what methods of pedagogy they use and what services they provide. Public schools must not exclude children on the basis of race, sex, or disability status. But they can choose their own methods to deliver instruction and assess student progress. Parents who find an individual school's methods distasteful, or think they are inappropriate for their child, have no reason to choose the school. Though schools that rely on family choice (for example, charter schools) are reluctant to conclude that they cannot serve a student, it is nonetheless possible for an unhappy family to leave. Thus a school is not obligated to diversify its services to meet every taste, and it is able to focus on providing a coherent instructional program consistent with the promises it made to parents.

Family choice strengthens schools in another way. It makes it possible for a school to say what levels of effort and attendance are required for success. If these are made explicit at the time of admission, a school has leverage to demand that parents and students fulfill their ends of the bargain.[10] This is not possible in a school that families have not chosen. The fact that a school of choice has made the same promises to all parents gives it leverage in dealing with children who decide they do not want to attend, work, or behave in ways agreed to upon admission. The school owes it to other children and parents not to permit erosion of its promised climate of respect, studiousness, and decorum. At the limit, a school of choice can conclude that a student has chosen, by failing to work and behave as promised, not to be a member of the school community.

Nothing can exempt public schools from the obligation to serve students of all income levels and ethnic groups. Public schools cannot expel students who will attend, try, and behave in ways that do not disrupt the education of others. However, if schools are to be held accountable for student outcomes, they must be free to uphold minimum standards of diligence on the parts of parents and students. If a school is to be truly accountable for results, it must be able to require responsible behavior from everyone, and it cannot permanently shield anyone from the consequences of his or her own actions. Students must be given many chances to succeed, but that does not mean that schools struggling to meet standards should bear the burden of some students' unwillingness to attend school, do work fairly assigned, or respect the learning opportunities of others.

This will be a troubling conclusion for people who understandably fear that schools will make arbitrary use of the freedom provided by family choice. Government authorizers must ensure that schools make and keep their promises about equitable student admission and retention policies. But consider the alternative: Schools that have no leverage to require student effort (and family support for effort and attendance) and cannot protect their instructional climates against serious disruption cannot realistically be held responsible for whether students learn.

RECIPROCAL TEACHER-SCHOOL CHOICE.   Teacher-school choice also promotes school performance accountability. Schools that need to attract teachers must make promises about working conditions and the quality and diligence of colleagues. A school that keeps its promises becomes attractive to teachers. Such schools are far more able to deliver on their promises to parents and government authorizers than schools that have no choice about whom they employ.

To a degree, teacher choice makes schools competitors. Schools that manage their teacher hiring or do not sustain a good professional climate will lose teachers and find it hard to deliver on their promises to parents. In situations where good teachers are in short supply, such competition could produce many losers. However, as the early experience of charter schools has shown, many talented individuals who do not want to teach in schools that have no control over their climate or instructional programs want to teach in schools that have significant freedom of action. Caroline M. Hoxby and Julia Koppich and Margaret Plecki have shown that many public school teachers who chose early retirement have returned to teach in charter schools.[11] Moreover, many highly educated young people who never before considered teaching are joining charter school faculties.

Thus reciprocal teacher-school choice can facilitate accountability in two ways: by strengthening individual schools as organizations able to deliver on their promises about instruction, and by improving the pool of potential teachers from which schools choose.

RELATIONSHIPS WITH INDEPENDENT DONORS AND SUPPORTERS. Help from independent parties can strengthen schools. Though school districts try to provide everything from advice to new instructional materials, and to keep physical plants in working condition, they often fail to meet schools' needs. Bureaucratic organization begets standardization. Schools benefit if they can get what they need from the district. Schools suffer if they need something that the district cannot offer, or if they need help more urgently than the district can provide it.

A school that is serious about providing an effective instructional program has no choice but to rely on sources other than its school district, at least some of the time. Most schools receive donations of all kinds from many sources including teachers and parents. Only schools whose parents and faculty have no contacts in the broader community do entirely without donations from independent sources.[12]

Moreover, the more clearly schools are held accountable for performance, the more they need, and seek, independent assistance. That is true of conventional public schools that come under scrutiny for low performance and of charter schools that face performance challenges. Schools of all kinds seek cash donations so that they can purchase assistance and materials, and they enter relationships with independent parties that can help them.

Such relationships are necessary, and there is no denying that they affect accountability. Schools that rely on independent providers and donors become accountable to them in some way. On the whole, an accountability relationship with an independent donor or provider reinforces a school's instructional program and thus its performance. Based on the evidence regarding the charter school experience, for-profit providers likely will seek to maximize efficiencies and profits to benefit stockholders. However, paired with effective oversight from authorizers and governing boards, for-profit providers also have strong incentives to demonstrate the value of their services. As with any provider, the question that school leaders and government overseers must ask is whether it contributes to school effectiveness.

Redefining Accountability in Public Education

Many states have committed themselves to the theory of standards-based reform without knowing how to make it work. How can officials in charge of the public school system tell the difference between schools that are low performing but on the road to improvement and those that are low performing and unlikely to improve? What can be done for children who are stuck in permanently low-performing schools? What freedoms do schools need if they are to be fairly held accountable for performance?

The answers to these questions must transform public oversight of schools. Until recently, states and school districts operated on the theory that if everyone's rights are protected and the inputs are well regulated, school quality will be the inevitable result. Standards-based reform makes accountability based on the inputs theory untenable. Command-and-control is replaced with a minimalist approach to regulation, one that relies as much as possible on problem solving by people who deliver services. Central determination is replaced by decentralized balancing. However, many states and districts are virtually clueless about how to oversee schools in this new environment. They will have to create capacities, in their own bureaucracies or school districts, or through independent vendors, to do many things few public agencies have ever done.

It is beyond the scope of this book to resolve the question of how government can play a more constructive role in public education. However, several well-thought-out proposals have been made about how the roles of states and school boards can be transformed in light of school-specific performance accountability.[13] The Education Commission of the States has suggested a way that compliance-oriented local school boards could be gradually replaced by new public oversight agencies with very different powers.[14]

However, we can conclude that charter schooling is the laboratory in which governments and schools can learn how to perform the functions implied by standards-based reform. Once considered odd and marginal, chartering can become, via the mechanism of standards-based reform, a template for public school accountability. Instead of being an alternative to standards-based reform, chartering can be the logical conclusion of it. Instead of being a barrier to charters, standards-based reform might be the route by which chartering becomes the normal way of providing public education.[15]

By making individual schools the locus of accountability, both standards-based reform and charter schools are leading a revolution in the public oversight of K–12 education. The charter school movement did not create the need to hold individual schools accountable for performance. That need has been recognized for decades by educators and policymakers who knew that compliance-based accountability weakened schools and diverted time and energy away from instruction.

Standards-based reform starts in a different place from chartering. But these different-looking proposals end up looking very much alike. If schools are to be accountable for whether students meet rigorous expectations, public oversight must focus on performance, not compliance and schools. Schools must have the freedom of action and control of resources that enable them to perform. A system of balanced accountability, in which schools are largely self-regulating and answer directly to families, teachers, donors, and government, can allow standards-based reform to fulfill its promise.

Notes

Chapter 1

1. For data and argument on different sides of these issues, see Amy Stuart Wells and others, "Charter Schools as Postmodern Paradox: Rethinking Social Stratification in an Age of Deregulated School Choice," *Harvard Educational Review*, vol. 69, no. 2 (Summer 1999), pp. 172–204; Richard Rothstein, "Charter Conundrum," *American Prospect* (July–August 1998); Bruce Fuller and others, *School Choice: Abundant Hopes, Scarce Evidence of Results* (Berkeley, Calif.: Policy Analysis for California Education, 1999); and Chester E. Finn, Bruno V. Manno, and Gregg Vanourek, *Charter Schools in Action: Renewing Public Education* (Princeton University Press, 2000).

2. Public Agenda, *On Thin Ice: How Advocates and Opponents Could Misread the Public's Views on Vouchers and Charter Schools* (New York: Public Agenda Foundation, 2000).

3. Terry E. Moe, "The New Economics of Organization," *American Journal of Political Science*, vol. 28, no. 4 (November 1984), pp. 739–77.

4. See, for example, Alan Altshuler, "Bureaucratic Innovation, Democratic Accountability, and Political Incentives," in Alan Altshuler and Robert D. Behn, eds., *Innovation in American Government, Challenges, Opportunities, and Dilemmas* (Brookings, 1997), pp. 38–67.

5. Terry E. Moe, "The Politics of Bureaucratic Structure," in John E. Chubb and Paul E. Peterson, eds., *Can the Government Govern?* (Brookings, 1989), pp. 267–329.

6. See, for example, Paul T. Hill, "The Federal Role in Education," in Diane Ravitch, ed., *Brookings Papers on Education Policy 2000* (Brookings, 2000), pp. 11–57.

7. Private sources of funding for this study are the Boeing Company, the Exxon Education Foundation, the Brookings Institution, and the Spencer Foundation.

8. Throughout this report we also make reference to schools or agencies (for example, Chicago and the District of Columbia school districts) visited in the course of other studies conducted by the authors.

9. For information on RPP International's study, see Paul Berman and others, *The State of Charter Schools: Third Year Report, National Study of Charter Schools 1999* (Department of Education, Office of Educational Research and Improvement, 1999).

10. Paul T. Hill, Robin Lake, and Mary Beth Celio, *A Study of Charter School Accountability*, final report submitted to the Department of Education, Contract #RC97110302, September 30, 1999.

Chapter 2

1. Mary Beth Celio, *Random Acts of Kindness? External Resources Available to the Seattle Public Schools* (University of Washington, Center on Reinventing Public Education, April 1996).

2. Anthony S. Bryk and others, *Charting Chicago School Reform* (Boulder, Colo.: Westview Press, 1998), chapter 7.

3. Note that California's law has changed since our study and looks more like a new supply law now.

4. See Paul Berman and others, *The State of Charter Schools: Third Year Report, National Study of Charter Schools 1999* (Department of Education, Office of Educational Research and Improvement, 1999), pp. 111–15.

Chapter 3

1. Fred M. Newmann, Bruce M. King, and Mark Rigdon, "Accountability and School Performance: Implications from Restructuring Schools," *Harvard Education Review*, vol. 67, no. 1 (Spring 1997), pp. 41–74.

2. Newmann, King, and Rigdon, "Accountability and School Performance."

3. Karl E. Weick, "Educational Organizations as Loosely Coupled Systems," *Administrative Science Quarterly*, vol. 21, no. 1 (March 1976), pp. 1–19. As Weick has observed, schools (and other professional organizations such as law firms and medical clinics) rely heavily on the expert judgment of individuals who practice, at least much of the time, on their own. Dependency on individual ex-

pertise means that such organizations cannot be rigidly programmed and efforts to completely standardize practice are counterproductive.

4. Priscilla Wohlstetter and others make a similar point. See Priscilla Wohlstetter and Noelle Griffin, *Creating and Sustaining Learning Communities: Early Lessons from Charter Schools* (Philadelphia: Consortium for Policy Research in Education, 1997).

5. For more in-depth discussion of the life cycles of charter schools, see Susan J. Korash, "Charter Schools as Educational Reform: A Case Study of the Creation of Three Colorado Charter Schools," Ph.D. dissertation, University of Houston, College of Education, August 1998. See also Chester E. Finn and others, *The Birth Pains and Life Cycles of Charter Schools* (Indianapolis: Hudson Institute Charter Schools in Action Project, August 1997).

6. See John Carver, *Boards Make a Difference: A New Design for Leadership in Non-Profit and Public Organizations* (San Francisco: Jossey-Bass, 1990), p. 54.

7. David Osborne and Ted Gaebler, *Reinventing Government* (Basic Books, 1991).

8. See, for example, Paul Berman and others, *A Study of Charter Schools: Second Year Report, 1998* (Department of Education, Office of Educational Research and Improvement, 1998), p. 99.

9. Chester E. Finn, Bruno V. Manno, and Gregg Vanourek, *Charter Schools in Action: Renewing Public Education* (Princeton University Press, 2000).

10. RPP International asked each charter school in the initial years of its operation about the reasons parents chose the school. The principals' ratings of the importance of twenty-one possible reasons formed five orthogonal factors: (1) smallness, including items about small school and classroom size; (2) effective schools, including those items most often identified in education literature as aspects of effective schools, namely, an active role for parents, clear goals, a strong academic program, a nurturing environment, a value system, a safe environment, and high standards; (3) response to special needs, including provision of services for students with disabilities, specialized curriculum foci, and ungraded or multiage provisions; (4) structured environment, including dress or behavior codes and support for home schooling; and (5) flexibility, including extensive use of technology, a flexible school schedule, a longer school year, a cultural focus for the school, community service components, and an adaptive environment.

11. Based on a cluster analysis of survey responses, principals classify parents' desires for effective schools according to six characteristics: nurturing, safe, high quality, high standards, clear goals, and parent involvement.

12. See Julia Koppich, Patricia Holmes, and Margaret L. Plecki, *New Rules, New Roles? The Professional Work Lives of Charter School Teachers* (Washington: National Education Association, 1998), pp. 26–34.

13. Koppich, Holmes, and Plecki, *New Rules*, p. 23.

14. See, for example, Berman and others, *A Study of Charter Schools,* p. 108. Less than 10 percent of all charter schools, including new schools, reported difficulty hiring staff.

15. Finn, Manno, and Vanourek, *Charter Schools in Action,* chapter 2.

16. See Berman and others, *A Study of Charter Schools,* pp. 106–09. Nearly 20 percent of charter schools reported problems with internal conflicts.

17. For information about charter approval and start-up, see Marc Dean Millot and Robin Lake, *So You Want to Start a Charter School? Strategic Advice for Applicants,* Recommendations from an Expert Workshop (University of Washington, Center on Reinventing Public Education, 1996). See also Finn and others, *The Birth Pains and Life Cycles of Charter Schools;* and Paul Berman and others, *The State of Charter Schools: Third Year Report* (Department of Education, Office of Educational Research and Improvement, 1999), pp. 41–54.

18. The Arizona State Board of Education employs two staff members to oversee their fifty-five charter schools. Charter schools are only a small part of the responsibilities of the state board, which also establishes educational policy for all schools in Arizona. The state board of education has tried to tighten its application process, but once a charter is awarded, it does little more than monitor the schools for compliance. Boxes of paper three and four feet high line the walls of the state office, and the director acknowledged that she had only physically visited about half (twenty-nine of fifty-five) of the schools. Usually the problem schools got the visits, that is, the schools that parents complained about. She generally conducted these visits on her own, and they were informal in nature. Surprisingly, she said that she could only "recommend" that a school take certain corrective actions, but that her office had "no teeth" to force compliance.

19. Ironically, the Arizona State Board of Education charter school director acknowledged that the 35th percentile cutoff was arbitrary and not an accurate reflection of a school's performance, especially a school that is serving at-risk students. However, she acknowledged that this was a rough attempt by the board to get a sense of how these schools were performing.

20. For an analysis of an authorizer that took its charter oversight responsibilities seriously, see Scott Hamilton, "Accountability in a World of Vouchers and Charter Schools," paper prepared for delivery at the Harvard University seminar on Vouchers and Choice, Cambridge, Mass., March 9–10, 2000.

21. *Charter Schools Today: Changing the Face of American Education* (Washington: Center for Education Reform, 2000).

22. For an account of how low-performing public schools in a standards-based reform state respond to ominously low scores on state standards-based tests, see Robin J. Lake and Paul T. Hill, *Making Standards Work* (Washington: Thomas J. Fordham Foundation, 1999).

23. See Anthony S. Bryk, Valerie C. Lee, and Peter B. Holland, *Catholic Schools and the Common Good* (Harvard University Press, 1993); Paul T. Hill, Gail E.

Fostrer, and Tamar Gendler, *High Schools with Character* (Santa Monica, Calif.: RAND, 1990); and James S. Coleman and Thomas Hoffer, *Public and Private High Schools: The Impact of Communities* (Basic Books, 1987).

Chapter 4

1. Judith Vitzthum's extraordinary work conducting the authorizer survey, and obtaining a 100 percent response rate, made an indispensable contribution to this study.

2. The Stanford-9 was the test most commonly required.

3. Paul Berman and others, *A Study of Charter Schools: Second Year Report, 1998* (Department of Education, Office of Educational Research and Improvement, 1998).

4. For a different, but complementary, typology of authorizing agencies, see Sandra Vergari, "The Regulatory Styles of Statewide Charter School Authorizers: Arizona, Massachusetts, and Michigan," *Educational Administration Quarterly*, vol. 36, no. 5 (December 2000), pp. 730–57.

Chapter 5

1. Traditional public schools receive donations and grants, and some develop long-term relationships with outside organizations (for example, schools that partner with industries that might then hire some of their graduates, such as schools affiliated with the Coalition for Essential Schools). These schools often take on many of the characteristics of charter schools. They are not solely accountable to their local school board, and they often find ways around constraints that apply to other schools (for example, hiring teachers who fit their programs, instead of accepting whatever the local civil service system gives them, or using the influence of their outside partners to resist the district's efforts to transfer their principals to other schools).

For the most part, however, traditional public schools enter temporary grantee and vendor arrangements that do not create long-term relationships of mutual dependency. They get a one-time grant from a business or foundation and expect to find another donor when the grant expires. They hire a consultant for a particular professional development session but do not expect a continuing relationship. Many traditional public schools are increasing their ties to these outside entities as their districts allow them more control over their budgets and encourage them to be more entrepreneurial (for example, in the Seattle school district). But these organizations normally have little or no stake in the success or failure of the school's overall academic program.

2. Paul Herdman and Marc Dean Millot, *Are Charter Schools Getting More Money into the Classroom? A Microfinancial Analysis of First Year Charter Schools in Massachusetts* (University of Washington, Center on Reinventing Public Education, October 2000).

3. Lynn Schnaiberg, "An Apparent First: Colorado Charter School Gets S&P Rating," *Education Week* (July 14, 1999).

4. Some schools with close ties to an authorizing or nearby district purposefully stay away from charter school associations or networks to ensure a good relationship with the district. Two schools we studied complement their districts by serving students that the district traditionally struggled to educate. For this reason, they have fairly friendly relationships with their nearby districts and do not want to jeopardize them by joining activist associations.

5. Amy Stuart Wells and Janelle Scott, *Beyond the Rhetoric of Charter School Reform: A Study of Ten California School Districts* (UCLA School of Education, 1999).

6. "Private School Choice Target in New Round of Court Challenge," *Education Week* (August 4, 1999).

7. Margaret Lin and Bryan Hassel, *Charting a Clear Course: A Resource Guide for Building Successful Partnerships between School Management Companies and School Management Organizations* (Washington: Charter Friends National Network, 1999).

8. Ted Kolderie, "States Begin to Withdraw the Exclusive," mimeo, 1992; and Joe Nathan, *Charter Schools: Creating Hope and Opportunity for American Education* (San Francisco: Jossey-Bass Publishers, 1996).

Chapter 6

1. These ideas are fully developed in John Brandl, *Money and Good Intentions Are Not Enough* (Brookings, 1998).

2. David Osborne and Ted Gaebler, *Reinventing Government* (Basic Books, 1991).

3. See, for example, Chester E. Finn, Bruno V. Manno, and Gregg Vanourek, *Charter Schools in Action: Renewing Public Education* (Princeton University Press, 2000), Appendix A.

Chapter 7

1. Analysts differ on who should bear the consequences of government's failure to fulfill its responsibilities under charters and standards-based reform. Amy Stuart Wells and Richard Rothstein, for example, caution against the expansion of charter schools, not because of the schools' failures but because of the failures

of public oversight. The trouble with this argument is that it allows opponents of charter schools in the school boards and central offices to thwart the development of charter schools by selectively and unilaterally deciding to ignore their oversight responsibilities. See Amy Stuart Wells and others, "Charter Schools as Postmodern Paradox: Rethinking Social Stratification in an Age of Deregulated School Choice," *Harvard Educational Review*, vol. 69, no. 2 (Summer 1999), pp.172–204. See also Richard Rothstein, "Charter Conundrum," *American Prospect* (July–August 1998).

2. Richard F. Elmore, *Leadership of Large-Scale Improvement in American Education* (Washington: Albert Shanker Institute, 1999), p. 5.

3. Standards-based reform expressly identifies local school district boards as the state agency responsible for direct school oversight. Though some charter school laws identify other possible public authorizers, every charter law empowers local districts to charter schools.

4. The arguments in this section are drawn from a larger analysis of the requirements of accountability under standards-based reform. See Sarah Brooks, *The Strong Schools Model of Accountability: Lessons for States Designing Standards-Based Reform* (University of Washington, Center on Reinventing Public Education, 2000).

5. Anthony S. Bryk and others, *Improving Community School Connections: Moving toward a System of Community Schools* (Baltimore: Annie E. Casey Foundation, 1999).

6. Lynn Olson, "Worries of a Standards 'Backlash' Grow," *Education Week* (April 5, 2000).

7. Bryan Hassel and Paul Herdman, *A Guide to Issues and Options for Charter Authorizers* (Charlotte, N.C.: Public Impact, 2001).

8. See, for example, Linda Brown, *The Massachusetts Charter School Handbook* (Boston: Pioneer Institute, 2000); D.C. Appleseed Center, *Charter Schools in the District of Columbia: Improving Systems for Accountability, Autonomy, and Competition* (Washington: D.C. Public Center School Board, 2001); and Marc Dean Millot and Robin Lake, *So You Want to Start a Charter School? Strategic Advice for Applicants*, Recommendations from an Expert Workshop (University of Washington, Center on Reinventing Public Education, 1996).

9. Sarah Brooks, *How States Can Hold Schools Accountable: The Strong Schools Model of Standards-Based Reform* (University of Washington, Center on Reinventing Public Education, 2000).

10. For a more elaborate development of this point, see Paul T. Hill, "The Educational Consequences of Choice," *Phi Delta Kappan* (June 1996), p. 671.

11. Caroline M. Hoxby, "Would School Choice Change the Teaching Profession?" Working Paper 7866 (Cambridge, Mass.: National Bureau of Economic Research, August 2000); and Julia Koppich and Margaret Plecki, *New Roles,*

New Rules? The Professional Lives of Charter School Teachers (Washington: Center for Advancement of Public Education, 1998).

12. See, for example, Mary Beth Celio, *Random Acts of Kindness? External Resources Available to the Seattle Public Schools* (University of Washington, Center for Reinventing Public Education, April 1996).

13. National Commission on Governing America's Schools, *Governing America's Schools: Changing the Rules* (Denver, Colo.: Education Commission of the States, 1999). See also Paul T. Hill, Lawrence C. Pierce, and James W. Guthrie, *Reinventing Public Education: How Contracting Can Transform America's Schools* (University of Chicago Press, 1997); and Chester E. Finn, Bruno V. Manno, and Gregg Vanourek, *Charter Schools in Action: Renewing Public Education* (Princeton University Press, 2000).

14. See Lawrence Pierce and others, *Bending without Breaking* (Denver, Colo.: Education Commission of the States, 1996).

15. For an excellent analysis of how an all-charter district or a district designed around standards-based reform would operate, see Finn, Manno, and Vanourek, *Charter Schools in Action.*

Index

Accountability: definition of, 5–6; democratic accountability, 6, 7–9; demonstration of student learning, 2; internal and external accountability, 25–26, 28; law and implementation, 14; mixed accountability, 85; standards, 100; theories of, 10–11, 85–86, 105. *See also* Authorizing agencies; Laws and politics

Accountability—charter schools: authorizers and, 41–42; autonomy and, 63–64, 66; conversion schools, 29–31; definition of, 13; development of, 26–31, 101; donors and funding, 64–69, 71; education management organizations, 75; effects of, 69–80; to families, 34–38; to government, 80; implementation, 13–14; improvement of, 88–96; internal and external accountability, 24–46, 71, 75, 86–88, 89; laws and political issues, 8–9, 21, 22–23; learning from, 97–109; multidirectional, 86–87, 97, 104; networks and, 69; outside organizations, 69–72, 77; performance agreements, 4–5, 6–7, 10; pressures for, 7, 45; reciprocity, 36–37; researchers, 73; responsibilities, 1, 3–4; rules and regulations, 13–17, 21–22; school governing boards and, 31–34; theory of, 10–11, 17–19, 26; unresolved issues, 86–87; voluntary associations, 64–69

Accountability—public education: balanced, 104–08, 109; consequences of new accountability, 9–12; meaning of, 5–7; national debate, 2; redefining, 108–09; at school level, 2–3; standards and standards-based reform, 100, 101, 105–06; teacher-school choice, 107–08

reviews and audits, 81, 82–83;
typical tensions of, 13–14
Legal and insurance issues, 67, 70
Leona Group, 74, 75
Los Angeles, 57

Magnet schools. *See* Public schools
and education
Management: education management
organizations, 64, 72, 74–75, 77–
78; for-profit management
companies, 70, 72–73; mission
and methods, 25; school
governing boards and, 78
Manno, Bruno V., 35
Massachusetts: accountability, 19,
59, 101, 103–04; advancements
in, 87; authorizers, 54, 59; Board
of Education (MBOE), 54, 59, 82;
conflict and crises, 45;
Department of Education, 82;
grants or donations, 66; oversight,
82–83, 84, 92; school governing
boards, 33; special needs students,
83; state assistance to charter
schools, 11–12, 84
Methodology, 11, 12
Michigan: accountability, 19, 82;
advancements in, 87; authorizers,
44–45, 54; charter expiration and
renewal, 41, 44–45; Department
of Education, 93; divisions
between elected officials, 12;
educational management
organizations, 75; National
Heritage Academies, 75; parent
and teacher education, 36, 91;
rules and regulations, 16; school
governing boards, 32–33. *See also*
Central Michigan University
Moe, Terry E., 8

National Association of Charter
School Authorizers, 104
National Heritage Academies
(NHA), 67, 75
New American Schools, 69
Newmann, Fred M., 25
New York City, 120–03
NHA. *See* National Heritage
Academies
North Carolina, 101
North Central Association of
Colleges and Schools, 68–69

Osborne, David, 34, 89

Parents: accommodation of, 37–38;
choice of charter schools, 19, 34,
35, 91, 113n10, 113n11;
complaints of, 8, 52, 56; focus of,
25, 72, 91; frequent shoppers, 35;
low-income and minority parents,
38; participation of, 36; pressures
on charter schools and, 3, 16–17,
24, 76; as principals in public
education, 6, 7, 11; reciprocal
accountability, 36–37; on school
governing boards, 32–33; school
leaders and, 36; view of charter
schools, 4, 27, 31, 34–35; in
voucher systems, 99; withdrawal
of children from charter schools,
35. *See also* Families
Plecki, Margaret L. 38–39, 107
Political issues. *See* Laws and
political issues
Private schools: conversion to charter
schools, 43; internal
accountability, 27; networks of,
17; school governing boards,
34, 89
Public debate, 2, 4